FAITH
IN THE
FAIRWAY

BUBBA WATSON   ZACH JOHNSON
STEWART CINK   DAVIS LOVE III
WEBB SIMPSON   LEE JANZEN
BEN CRANE, GENERAL EDITOR

HARVEST HOUSE PUBLISHERS
EUGENE, OREGON

A list of Scripture versions quoted in this book is included at the back.

Cover by Harvest House Publishers Inc., Eugene, Oregon

Cover photo © nicholashan / iStock

FAITH IN THE FAIRWAY
Copyright © 2014 by the Ben and Heather Crane Foundation
Published by Harvest House Publishers
Eugene, Oregon 97402
www.harvesthousepublishers.com

Library of Congress Cataloging-in-Publication Data
   Faith in the fairway / Ben Crane, general editor.
      pages cm
   ISBN 978-0-7369-6249-0 (pbk.)
   ISBN 978-0-7369-6248-3 (eBook)
   1. Golfers—Prayers and devotions. 2. Golfers—Religious life. 3. Golf—Religious aspects—
Christianity. I. Crane, Ben, 1976- editor.
   BV4596.G64F35 2014
   242'.68—dc23

2014021864

Printed in the United States of America

18 19 20 21 22 / VP-CD / 10 9 8 7 6 5 4

Contributors

(in alphabetical order)

Aaron Baddeley

Jonathan Byrd

Stewart Cink

Ben Crane, General Editor

Lee Janzen

Zach Johnson

Tom Lehman

Justin Leonard

Davis Love III

Webb Simpson

Scott Stallings

Kevin Streelman

Cameron Tringale

Bubba Watson

Mark Wilson

God is great, so we don't have to control everything ourselves.

I'm a perfectionist. Golf is not the best game to play when plagued with this condition. In my first tournament last year, I wasn't hitting the ball the way I wanted to on Saturday. That afternoon, I walked off the course thinking my game probably wasn't going to be good enough to win. Typically, I would head to the range, but instead, I went and hit a few putts and decided to just let it go. Strangely, I rested and believed I didn't have to be perfect to win this tournament…and oddly enough, it was true! I won! I prepared well, but I couldn't completely control my game. I realized that complete control of a game with many variables is impossible.

Whatever I treasure the most will control my heart. Whatever controls my heart will control my behavior. May God be my treasure. He *is* big enough.

What things do you treasure most in your life? How might they be controlling you?

Do you need to loosen your grip on anything today?

God, help me treasure you today, and help me relax my white-knuckled grip on a few things that I can't control anyway.

—Jonathan Byrd

Everyone who drinks of this water will be thirsty again, but whoever drinks of the water that I give him will never be thirsty again.

God is good, so we don't have to look elsewhere.

During the off-season I work hard, prepare well, and plan expectantly for a good upcoming season. Last year, my diligence paid off with my best year ever on the PGA Tour. After reflecting on the year, however, I still wasn't satisfied. Most often I left the course wishing I had played better and realizing I had lost numerous opportunities. My best golf year didn't fulfill me the way I thought it would. Why?

God has made each of us with a bigger thirst than anything the world can fill. He is the only one who can satisfy. Enjoy golf and work hard at it, but in the end, let it go! It's a wonderful game, but a horrible god. God is perfectly good!

What would a fulfilling life look like to you?

How can you find your fulfillment in God?

Heavenly Father, I'm thankful for the incredible life you've given me. Help me to never let the blessings in my life become distractions from what's most important.

—Jonathan Byrd

Scripture Reading: Psalm 103:8, 10,14 ESV

The LORD is merciful and gracious, slow to anger and abounding in steadfast love…He does not deal with us according to our sins, nor repay us according to our iniquities… He knows our frame; he remembers that we are dust.

God is gracious, so we don't need to prove ourselves to him.

I sat in the locker room on Wednesday at the first tournament of the season, the Hyundai Tournament of Champions. On each player's locker was a list of his tournament wins during the previous year, including some majors. I began to compare my record to the other players', and suddenly mine didn't seem to measure up. I wondered, "Am I as good as the other players in this tournament?" I began to fall into the trap of believing that I needed to prove myself. Prove that I deserved to be there, that my win wasn't just a fluke. Soon the joy I had felt leading up to this prestigious event faded, and I was left anxious and stressed.

I had embraced a lie! I don't need to prove myself. God loves me, and he saved me in the middle of my sin through his gracious work in Christ. Remembering this truth freed me up to compete well. I wasn't bound by any expectations any longer. With joy and freedom, I could enjoy my previous year's success and my Savior's love.

Are you trying to prove yourself today—to yourself, your family, your coworkers?

Do you tend to compare yourself to anyone? Who? What do you think God has to say about that?

Lord, I believe you love me, and that's enough for me. I don't have to prove my worth to anybody because you've demonstrated that I'm valuable to you.

—Jonathan Byrd

Scripture Reading: Proverbs 3:6 NASB

In all your ways acknowledge Him, and He will make your paths straight.

Acknowledging God is the best thing we can do for ourselves and for others.

Our sinful nature tends to desire things that will give us an immediate advantage or a quick rush. How about enjoying a few too many desserts after dinner or talking about people behind their backs? These indulgences can feel good at the moment, but they will come back to hurt us. To live by God's objectives, we should be living to give God glory and to honor and care for others. Showing humility, caring for others, practicing patience... these are ways we can acknowledge God.

Have you ever seen someone acknowledge God in an extremely classy or winsome way? How did that person do it?

What behaviors can you do today to acknowledge God?

Lord, thank you for inviting me to work for your kingdom today.

—Mark Wilson

Scripture Reading: Job 2:10

Job replied… "Shall we accept good from God and not trouble?"

We always have reasons to give thanks to God.

Job was one of the richest men in his time, but he was suddenly stripped of his material wealth, his children, and his health. Job's perspective is admirable—he chose to accept life's blessings as well as its struggles, its highs and its lows. Do you ever thank God for a tough day because you know it could be enlightening to you in the future? My guess is that many of us thank God later on, when we have the whole story, but seldom do we thank him while the trouble is happening.

We can pray to him about areas in our lives that we consider tough right now—our careers, our relationships with our family, or whatever—and genuinely thank him for the opportunity to grow. That sounds hard to do, but as we cooperate with him, he will give us strength to give thanks in all circumstances.

Consider memorizing 1 Thessalonians 5:16-18: "Rejoice always, pray continually, give thanks in all circumstances; for this is God's will for you in Christ Jesus."

Develop an attitude of gratitude for your life story.

God, help me to look to you in every circumstance in my life, and empower me to always give you thanks.

—Mark Wilson

Scripture Reading: Colossians 3:12

As God's chosen people, holy and dearly loved, clothe yourselves with compassion, kindness, humility, gentleness and patience.

The male population can benefit from a lesson on compassion. Men have a tendency to reach for their toolbox and repair something that's broken. But when it comes to relationships, your wife isn't looking for a quick fix. She wants to be heard and validated. When your lady wants to tell you the challenging aspects of her day, turn off the TV and computer, look at her face, listen to her words, and feel what she is feeling. Resist the urge to point out a quick solution. She wants to hear you say, "I know what you mean," or "Me too." Don't tell her what she should have done. A compassionate husband nods his head and shares his wife's emotions whether they are painful or pleasant.

How can you jump into your significant other's shoes and walk around for a bit today?

What skills do you need to improve to be a better listener?

Lord, help me to see other people's perspective on things today and genuinely feel their viewpoint.

—Mark Wilson

My grade school principal reminded me often to be a walking sermon. That was a great reminder that people were paying attention to my behavior.

If you grumble and complain at work and people know you consider yourself a Christian, do you think they will want to get to know Jesus better? They probably won't because you aren't showing them a life that is desirable. On the other hand, if you are a person who is learning to see the glass as half full, to show a genuine concern for others, and to avoid judging them, people may want to figure out what you and God are all about. Your living example can speak volumes. Be infectious with your peace.

Even though it isn't essential to know Bible verses when witnessing, they sure can be comforting, so take a little time to memorize one verse about Jesus's saving grace, such as Romans 10:9.

What is one respectful way you can display your faith today?

God, may my hope in you guide my decisions today. Help me to be gentle and respectful in all my relationships so others will be drawn to you.

—Mark Wilson

Scripture Reading: 1 Corinthians 9:22-23 NLT

I try to find common ground with everyone, doing everything I can to save some. I do everything to spread the Good News and share in its blessing.

Everything passes away in this world except God and his Word. We are constantly communicating with other golfers, coworkers, neighbors, friends, and family. In doing so we have one goal—that they would know and walk with Christ. Paul gives us a clear depiction of how we are to encourage them to walk with the Lord. He tells us to actively look for common ground with those around us. We are all experts in our own stories, but are we caring enough about the people God has put right in front of us to engage in their stories? Today let's find common ground with people and encourage a friend we know as well as someone new.

Who comes to mind that you can encourage today? Is it your golfing partner? An estranged family member? Someone else? Let the Holy Spirit lead you to that person today.

If you want to experience a more abundant life, you must be actively engaged in finding common ground with those around you. Spend a few minutes in prayer now and ask the Lord how you can do this today.

God, when you became a man in Christ, you provided the ultimate example of finding common ground. I ask for wisdom, understanding, and sensitivity today so I can find common ground with people I meet.

—Ben Crane

Scripture Reading: Ecclesiastes 5:18-20; 6:9 NLT

It is good for people to eat, drink, and enjoy their work under the sun during the short life God has given them, and to accept their lot in life. And it is a good thing to receive wealth from God and the good health to enjoy it...God keeps such people so busy enjoying life that they take no time to brood over the past...Enjoy what you have rather than desiring what you don't have. Just dreaming about nice things is meaningless—like chasing the wind.

Compared to the vast majority of people on this planet, you are likely wealthy. Still, we all act as if we need more. I don't know about you, but if you ask me what is the next thing I want to buy, I can give you an immediate answer. It is a sickness and a discontent. Many of the most contented people I know actually have the smallest amount of worldly goods. Material possessions clearly do not breed contentment. In fact, we can actually make a better case for the opposite. We all know some very rich people who are miserable! Solomon tells us that riches can be beneficial if we accept them and use them, knowing that they are in fact a gift from God.

Larry Moody, who has been our chaplain on the PGA Tour for the past 30 years, tells us that if we own something that we can't give away, we don't own it—it owns us. Do you have any possessions that you couldn't give away? Name them!

What can you give away today that you know will mean more to someone else? It could be your time, your talent, or a treasure. Commit today to a friend or spouse to give it away.

Lord Jesus, author and perfecter of my life and Creator of all the good gifts in my life, take away my selfish desires and the part of me that thinks I need more.

—Ben Crane

When these Israelites heard the Law of Moses, they were overwhelmed because the Law was difficult, it exposed their imperfections, and obeying it would require them to change some of their current behavior.

When we study the Word of God, either in church, at a Bible study, or on our own, we sometimes feel overwhelmed as God's laws expose our own shortcomings. We may feel as if God is asking us to do the impossible, but all things are possible with him. When God exposes our hearts through his Word, his intent is not to make us feel guilty, but to lead us to greater joy and freedom.

If you had only a short elevator ride to share the gospel, how would you do it? What would you say?

Do any of God's laws and commands seem impossible for you to obey today?

God, your Word teaches that your commands are not burdensome and that when we believe, we overcome. Empower me to maintain that confidence today and to walk in joyful obedience.

—Cameron Tringale

Scripture Reading: Luke 7:22-23

[Jesus] replied to the messengers, "Go back and report to John what you have seen and heard: The blind receive sight, the lame walk, those who have leprosy are cleansed, the deaf hear, the dead are raised, and the good news is proclaimed to the poor. Blessed is anyone who does not stumble on account of me."

When John the Baptist was in prison, he began to doubt Jesus. Like John, we tend to doubt God when things are not going well in our lives. We must remember that our personal circumstances do not necessarily coincide with the way God feels about us, and we must not let our faith hang on what God is or isn't doing in us or for us. God proved his feelings for us at the cross. When we experience tough times, we need to recount all the amazing times God has come through for us and blessed us instead of selfishly doubting him. Jesus tells us we will be blessed when we are faithful to God in the tough times.

Recall a time when you were tempted to doubt God because of your personal circumstances. Did you give in to doubt, or did you recall the blessings you've received?

Do you know someone who is doubting God because of tough times? Start praying for that person today.

God, I confess that I am prone to doubt. I choose today to look to the cross—not to my circumstances—as evidence of your great love for me.

—Cameron Tringale

Scripture Reading: Acts 2:38-41

Peter replied, "Repent and be baptized, every one of you, in the name of Jesus Christ for the forgiveness of your sins. And you will receive the gift of the Holy Spirit. The promise is for you and your children and for all who are far off—for all whom the Lord our God will call." With many other words he warned them; and he pleaded with them, "Save yourselves from this corrupt generation." Those who accepted his message were baptized, and about three thousand were added to their number that day.

Here are two amazing things about God: He relentlessly pursues us, and he wants to have a personal relationship with each and every one of us.

I love this reminder that the promise of salvation—the good news of the gospel—is for everyone. Even though we're all imperfect, we can rejoice because Jesus died for our sins—our imperfections—so we could know God and have new life in him.

How did you feel when you first realized God would accept you and give you the Holy Spirit just as you were?

Do you know anyone who is "far off" and needs to hear the good news of the Lord?

Lord, help me to always be amazed by your relentless love.

—Cameron Tringale

Scripture Reading: James 1:2-4 ESV

Count it all joy, my brothers, when you meet trials of various kinds, for you know that the testing of your faith produces steadfastness. And let steadfastness have its full effect, that you may be perfect and complete, lacking nothing.

The old adage "What doesn't kill you, makes you stronger" must have been derived from this verse. At work, in sports, in relationships, and in faith, this statement rings true. Nobody enjoys the struggles that inevitably come with life on earth. But James tells us that we need to embrace the battles of life because when we endure, we become stronger. Whatever trial may come your way, God can use it to make you more like Jesus. To be steadfast is to be fixed and immovable. We can be perfect (mature) and complete (fully developed) in life only when we know Jesus.

Have you ever endured a tough time and come away stronger, feeling a closer relationship with God?

What trials are you facing today, and how can you embrace them and benefit from them?

Lord, I admit that sometimes I'd rather take the easy way out instead of letting steadfastness have its full effect. Today I choose to take the long view, trusting that you are helping me to become mature and fully developed.

—Cameron Tringale

Scripture Reading: Philippians 3:12-14,16

Not that I have already obtained all this, or have already arrived at my goal, but I press on to take hold of that for which Christ Jesus took hold of me. Brothers and sisters, I do not consider myself yet to have taken hold of it. But one thing I do: Forgetting what is behind and straining toward what is ahead, I press on toward the goal to win the prize for which God has called me heavenward in Christ Jesus…Let us live up to what we have already attained.

Paul studied the life of Jesus and probably knew more about him than anyone else has since. Paul isn't complacent, thinking he knows it all or has reached his goal. Instead, he is committed to continue pursuing Christ. Whether we are far along in our journey or new Christians, we need to proactively pursue deeper relationships with Jesus Christ. God will continue to grant us new insights, and we need to put that knowledge to work and apply it in our lives. After all, isn't that the point of learning to grow? As Paul says, we need to "live up to what we have already attained."

What realistic commitment can you make that will help you pursue the Lord on a daily basis?

Are any areas of your life out of step with your knowledge of God and his ways?

God, thank you for reminding me that I have a long way to go. You have taken hold of me, so I know you will empower me to reach the ultimate goal.

—Cameron Tringale

Scripture Reading: Colossians 1:11 NLT

We also pray that you will be strengthened with all his glorious power so you will have all the endurance and patience you need.

When the apostle Paul prayed for the faithful servants of Christ at Colossae, he revealed what God's glorious might provides for us.

Life on the road, time away from my family, playing a very frustrating and humbling game week after week, the pressure to perform...these things can tear me apart physically and mentally. You and I may not share these same circumstances, but we all go through our share of tough times. But God's mighty power will give us the strength to endure the physical grind and the patience to endure the mental grind day in day out. Life isn't a sprint, but rather a marathon. All we truly need is to look to God for the strength to reach the finish line.

What challenges do you face this week?

How can you appropriate God's glorious power for the patience and endurance you need?

Lord, fill my body, mind, and spirit with your glorious strength so I have the patience and endurance to press through the marathon of life. All power comes from you—thanks be to God!

—Zach Johnson

Scripture Reading: Genesis 1:11 NLT

Then God said, "Let the land sprout with vegetation—every sort of seed-bearing plant, and trees that grow seed-bearing fruit. These seeds will then produce the kinds of plants and trees from which they came." And that is what happened.

This week, a wise man challenged me to go out onto the golf course simply to enjoy a nice walk in the park. To enjoy exactly what God intended for us from the very beginning—quiet moments with him in his beautiful creation. We can easily get caught up in the monotony of the week, taking for granted the beauty God has laid before our feet and eyes. He is the Creator of everything and wants us to find joy in all that he has given us.

We all take God's gift of creation for granted at times. Today capture some mental pictures of what you see and take delight in the fact that our Lord is the Creator of all.

What does creation reveal to you about God?

Lord, maker of heaven and earth, thank you for the beauty of your creation. Help me to never take your incredible gifts for granted, but rather to look forward to my walks in the park with you.

—Zach Johnson

Scripture Reading: Romans 1:5 NLT

Through Christ, God has given us the privilege and authority as apostles to tell Gentiles everywhere what God has done for them, so that they will believe and obey him, bringing glory to his name.

This is Paul's mission statement—he lived to spread the good news. We, too, are to look for any opportunity to tell what God has done through the resurrection of his Son, Christ Jesus. We are responsible to grab hold of every opportunity to glorify his name, leading others along the way. We may not be apostles, but Jesus has commissioned us.

In golf, each shot, every hole, each round, and every tournament is an opportunity to show greatness. In our daily walk, every day, every relationship, every encounter, and every engagement is an opportunity to show God's grace. Paul wants us to make the most of these opportunities.

Can you share the good news of God's work with someone today? Pray for God to reveal that person to you, and pray for the Holy Spirit to direct your words and actions along the way.

Always be on alert for an opportunity to share the Word, knowing full well you have been called to do so. Our Lord is pleased when we can glorify his holy name.

God, help me to be a man on a mission to share the tremendous news of your great love for everyone.

—Zach Johnson

This is a life passage to many, including me. Some of the finest words of wisdom I have been given relate to this proverb. As Christians, our goal in life should be to depend completely on Christ. All that we do, all that we say, how we interact, how we live…everything should reflect the fact that we have a relationship with the true, living God. Each and every day, let's let the Lord drive our motives, our actions, and our decisions so that we are looking up rather than simply looking in the mirror.

What might be the difference between making smart decisions (which we must do) and depending on our own understanding (which Proverbs counsels us not to do)?

What decision are you facing today? What does trusting the Lord mean to you in your current situation?

Lord, I cannot tackle today or tomorrow without you. I put my trust in you to lead me down the road you have chosen for me. Open my heart so your Holy Spirit is all that I depend on, all that I rely on, all my days.

—Zach Johnson

Throw off your old sinful nature and your former way of life, which is corrupted by lust and deception. Instead, let the Spirit renew your thoughts and attitudes. Put on your new nature, created to be like God—truly righteous and holy.

In the first sentence in today's passage (verse 22), the apostle Paul urges us to quit acting the way we used to act. In the last sentence (verse 24), he encourages us to live according to our new nature, just as God created us to. The middle sentence (verse 23) is the bridge—in order to become more like Christ, we constantly have to be renewed in our thoughts. Whatever we are thinking is eventually what we will say or do, so we strive to replace the old attitude with a Christlike attitude every day.

What unhelpful thoughts constantly try to creep into your mind?

What are some fresh, positive thoughts you can use to replace them?

Lord, give me the strength and determination to change my thoughts and attitudes and to renew my mind.

—Davis Love III

Do not lie to each other, since you have taken off your old self with its practices and have put on the new self, which is being renewed in knowledge in the image of its Creator.

To "put on the new self" as a Christian is to let our faith determine the way we think and act. Regardless of what we say or do, God knows what we think and feel. Paul is saying that good intentions aren't enough—we must also have the right actions.

Are you surprised that Paul would have to tell the Christians at Colossae not to lie to each other? The Bible doesn't pull any punches when describing our unregenerate nature, and it doesn't sugarcoat the truth when talking about our everyday experience. But we can be thankful that the Bible writers were also unrelenting in their optimism—we really can live a new life!

Do your words reflect your faith? Commit yourself today to avoid lies (rumors, gossip, exaggeration) and maintain a reputation of honesty.

How can you show your faith to others today through what you say and do?

Dear Lord, continue to build my faith and renew my mind so my thoughts and actions will glorify you.

—Davis Love III

A friend sent me this verse when I needed motivation to read the Bible more consistently.

Our lives are busy—we all have many important responsibilities to fulfill, necessary tasks to complete, and wonderful opportunities to explore. But these must never distract us from eating our "daily bread" by reading the Bible. As we develop our appetite for Scripture, God's Word will increasingly become a joy for us and the delight of our hearts.

Is reading the Bible a chore for you, or do you "eat up" the words?

How can you breathe new life into your daily study this week?

Do you have a friend who needs some encouragement to read God's Word?

Lord, thank you for the gift of the Bible. Help me to go deeper in my study and to make the Bible a bigger part of my life.

—Davis Love III

Scripture Reading: 2 Corinthians 10:4-5 ESV

The weapons of our warfare are not of the flesh but have divine power to destroy strongholds. We destroy arguments and every lofty opinion raised against the knowledge of God, and take every thought captive to obey Christ.

Paul was just like us—as limited by human frailty as we are. But he didn't have to rely on human plans or methods to overcome the tremendous struggles in his life, and neither do we. God's weapons and strength are available to us to keep us strong when the world tries to drag us down. As Christians we must find our strength in prayer, faith, love, and the Holy Spirit.

What parts of your life are you tempted to control on your own without prayer or reliance on God's strength and wisdom?

What current struggle or decision can you turn over to God, relying on his strength?

Lord, thank you for our blessings and for your grace. Help me to look to you every day in all aspects of my life.

—Davis Love III

Scripture Reading: Psalm 27:4 NKJV

One thing I have desired of the LORD, that I will seek: that I may dwell in the house of the LORD all the days of my life, to behold the beauty of the LORD and to inquire in His temple.

Hear the cry of King David's heart. Even though he was a king, even though he had all the material possessions he could want, the number one thing he sought after was God. His heart's desire, his passion, was to dwell in the presence of God, to understand who this amazing God really is, and to live with him. Notice his ultimate desire was God himself and not what God could do for him. This is why God describes David as a man after his own heart.

What does "dwelling in God's presence" mean to you?

What are a couple of your greatest desires? How are those desires manifested in your life?

God, help me to learn more about you, to sense your presence in my life, to follow your lead...to make you my number one desire.

—Aaron Baddeley

Scripture Reading: James 4:8 NKJV

Draw near to God and He will draw near to you.

Dwell on the words of this Scripture. God is the Creator of the universe—the One who placed the stars in the sky and created the sun and the moon, the tranquil beaches and awe-inspiring mountains. He is inviting you to come close to him. God made you in his image because his ultimate desire is for you to walk closely with him. But he won't force the issue—God offers the invitation and leaves the response up to you.

What is your response to God's invitation? Are you initiating the contact or waiting on him?

Do you need to make any changes in order to draw near to God?

Lord, I desire to walk intimately with you. I believe this promise from your Word, that as I draw near to you, you will draw near to me. Thank you for loving me and choosing me.

—Aaron Baddeley

"Let not the wise man glory in his wisdom, let not the mighty man glory in his might, let not the rich man glory in his riches; but let him who glories glory in this, that he understands and knows Me, that I am the LORD, exercising lovingkindness, judgment, and righteousness in the earth. For in these I delight," says the LORD.

It doesn't take long for new Christians to realize that when we come to Christ, we need to get serious about changing the way we think. The values, priorities, and goals we grew up with aren't likely to match what we find in Scripture.

What new ways of thinking do we find in the Bible? First, we are to be grateful that we can know God, his greatness, and his never-ending love. Second, we are to gratefully receive the resurrection power of his Son Jesus Christ.

Do you ever realize you've talked a lot about what you have done and left God out of the picture? Read 2 Corinthians 12:9-10 and Galatians 6:14.

What have you recently learned about how great and wonderful and loving God is?

How can you cultivate a deeper relationship with him?

Lord, I confess that my concept of glory is often different from yours. Help me find true glory by learning more about you and living accordingly.

—Aaron Baddeley

Imagine a tree saying, "I don't need any rain or water—I'm good. I can manage on my own." That tree would surely wither and die.

The same is true for us when we try to live life apart from God, in our own strength. God created us to live in relationship with him—we were never meant to live apart from him. As we stay close to Jesus, relying on him, we remain healthy, strong, and fruitful. With him we can do all things.

What does "living in your own strength" mean to you?

What does "abiding in Christ" mean to you?

Read Mark 10:27 and Philippians 4:13.

Lord, thank you for providing everything I need to be the person you created me to be and to accomplish all you have given me to do.

—Aaron Baddeley

In Deuteronomy 6 we are told that the most effective "family altars," or devotional times, occur frequently, spontaneously, and naturally through the day as we share teaching moments with our children. These are times to be a spiritual leader to your kids. In the car, be their friend. At dinnertime, help them see their world from a biblical point of view. At bedtime, help them express their fears and problems, and reassure them of Christ's love and power in their lives. Make them feel safe.

What is one way you can demonstrate the truth to your kids today?

How would you describe authentic spiritual leadership in the family?

Lord, help me to be the dad my kids need and the husband my wife needs. May my words and my actions inspire, encourage, and comfort my family.

—Justin Leonard

Scripture Reading: Romans 8:28 NKJV

We know that all things work together for good to those who love God, to those who are called according to His purpose.

This is one of the greatest promises in the Bible, for it summarizes all the others. It is the foundation of our hope and confidence. Even our failures can become enriching and our sins can be forgiven. Our losses can prepare us for greater victories, and our pain can lead to deep joy. Even death itself becomes a blessing for the child of God.

The first part of the verse is the promise. The last half is the condition.

What difficult situation are you facing that God might be using for your ultimate good?

How can you demonstrate your love for God today?

God, I can't control every circumstance in my life, but I can choose to trust you. Thank you for loving me, for giving my life meaning and purpose, and for using "all things" for my ultimate good.

—Justin Leonard

Scripture Reading: Proverbs 15:1

A gentle answer turns away wrath, but a harsh word stirs up anger.

The book of Proverbs is packed with verses about our tempers and our tongues. This verse applies particularly to our tone of voice. It talks about a gentle answer and a harsh word. The adjectives "gentle" and "harsh" describe the way we are to speak as well as what we are to say.

A conversation may seem simple on the outside, but a multitude of hidden feelings and agendas can be hidden beneath the surface. When we are tempted to speak harshly, we do well to ask ourselves why we are so bothered. Perhaps somebody touched a nerve in us—a tender spot that could use Christ's healing touch.

Have you spoken a harsh word recently? What emotions prompted you to speak the way you did?

Would a "gentle answer" have been appropriate? How might you have worded it?

Lord, please guard my lips. Help me to treat others with special care, just as you do for me.

—Justin Leonard

Scripture Reading: James 1:3 NASB

The testing of your faith produces endurance.

Faith is like a muscle—it must be repeatedly tested if its strength and endurance are to increase. Tests and trials are rarely fun, and we may wonder, is the pain of testing worth the result? The answer is yes! God's goal for us is to become mature and complete, lacking nothing. The process may not always be easy, but life will be more meaningful and a lot more fun as we become the people God created us to be.

Endurance is the ability to undergo a period of stress and strain with the inner strength of Christ, emerging from it stronger than when we entered.

Praising God is easy during the good times. Can you thank him right now for a difficult test you've endured?

Are you facing a potentially discouraging circumstance? What could God possibly accomplish in and through you in this situation?

God, thank you for making me stronger and more like you. Help me to trust you even when I don't understand how you're using certain events in my life.

—Justin Leonard

Scripture Reading: Genesis 1:3

And God said, "Let there be light," and there was light.

When God speaks, big things happen.

God spoke all of creation into being. He probably could have created everything even without speaking, but when God does speak, we see his power. When Jesus was baptized and then again at the mount of transfiguration, people heard God's audible voice. His words encouraged Jesus and instructed others who heard them.

In James 3:1-12, we learn that our words have power too—for better or for worse! The words that come from our mouths can bless God one minute and curse man the next.

The words we say to ourselves can make a difference in our lives each day. The way we talk to ourselves can also determine how we talk to others. Let's make a habit of speaking words that are blessings in others' lives as well as in our own.

Think of someone you'll see today. What can you say to that person that will encourage him or her?

What words do you commonly say to yourself? If they are not encouraging, what might you say instead?

Lord, thank you for your Word. Help me choose the right words so I will be a blessing to others and to you.

—Lee Janzen

Scripture Reading: Luke 6:48 NET

He is like a man building a house, who dug down deep, and laid the foundation on bedrock. When a flood came, the river burst against that house but could not shake it, because it had been well built.

All golfers know that a good game results from mastering the basics. Good grip, stance, posture, aim, and ball position are all necessary for a solid foundation.

Our faith must rest on the solid foundation of Jesus Christ. When Jesus died for us, he paid the penalty for our sin. This is the foundation of our faith. It cannot be shaken, so we can have peace when life hits us like a flood. When we fall short in anything we do, we can remain confident that God will never give up on us. We'll never earn our way to heaven, so let's make sure we're anchored to the foundation of God's grace.

What kinds of floods might Jesus be referring to in today's verse? How can God's grace protect you in these floods?

How can you anchor yourself today to the foundation of God's grace?

Thank you, Lord, for the gift of grace. I know I can't earn my way to heaven, so help me to rest on the foundation of Jesus Christ during any trials in my life.

—Lee Janzen

Scripture Reading: John 16:33 NET

I have told you these things so that in me you may have peace. In the world you have trouble and suffering, but take courage—I have conquered the world.

Jesus comforted his disciples by telling them he has provided everything they would need.

We will always have troubles in our lives, but they will not keep us from eternal life. Jesus doesn't want us to focus on our troubles in this world, but on him and on heaven, which awaits us. Jesus has overcome every possible scenario that could separate us from him, so we can have peace here and now, even in our suffering.

Here is another reason we can have peace—even though trials are coming our way, we know they will pass. We can have courage to put ourselves in situations that normally make us uneasy. What could possibly happen? Jesus has overcome!

Sometimes we lose peace because we focus on the wrong things. The trials and suffering we face can be great—they naturally steal our attention. Have peace, knowing Jesus has acted on our behalf already. When an obstacle pops up, take courage and be an overcomer!

Jesus has conquered the world—how might that give you courage?

What troubles are you facing? Imagine yourself walking through a difficult experience with the peace of Jesus.

Thank you, Jesus, for overcoming all things, including death. Remind me to always find peace in you.

—Lee Janzen

Scripture Reading: Psalm 46:10 NET

Stop your striving and recognize that I am God! I will be exalted over the nations! I will be exalted over the earth!

He is God. We are not.

We can't do anything to change God's plans or stop what he's doing. We may have some influence in our relationships, and the things we do may make a difference in other people's lives, but these things don't change God's ultimate plans.

We also can't earn a better standing with God. Our accomplishments may bring praise from other people, but what can we do that could possibly impress God? Nothing we can do could make him love us more, and nothing we can do could make him love us less.

So instead of muscling our way through life or trying to impress God or other people, we can rest assured that God has accepted us and that he is all we will ever need.

In what ways are you sometimes striving in life?

Whisper these words: "You are God. I am not." How might that change your outlook on today?

Lord, thank you for giving me air to breathe. If I lose all that I have, I still have you, and you're all I need.

—Lee Janzen

Scripture Reading: 1 Timothy 1:12 NLT

I thank Christ Jesus our Lord, who has given me strength to do his work. He considered me trustworthy and appointed me to serve him.

We have not arrived at this time and place by accident. The foundations of our faith and the platforms we have been given are not the results of luck or chance. God has appointed us to use our gifts to serve and worship him. We must remember to constantly acknowledge, praise, and thank the Lord who has appointed us to serve him—the one, true King!

List three things you have accomplished. Thank God for each one as a blessing from him.

God has blessed you with a unique platform. How can you use it to honor and serve him today?

Father, thank you for giving me the platform and the strength to cooperate with your work in the world. I consider it an honor, and I strive to please you in all I do. Please be with me today and use my abilities and blessings to represent your kingdom wherever I can.

—Kevin Streelman

Scripture Reading: Romans 8:38-39 NLT

I am convinced that nothing can ever separate us from God's love. Neither death nor life, neither angels nor demons, neither our fears for today nor our worries about tomorrow—not even the powers of hell can separate us from God's love. No power in the sky above or in the earth below—indeed, nothing in all creation will ever be able to separate us from the love of God that is revealed in Christ Jesus our Lord.

God's immeasurable, perfect, and true love for us is undeserved. It is so beautiful that it's impossible to comprehend. In God's love, he sent his Son to die for us so we could be reunited with him. How reassuring it is to know that there is nothing on this earth, under it, or above it that will ever be able to take his love away from us!

Are any deep fears and doubts hidden in your heart and mind? What can you do to rely on God's love to provide all you need in these trying times?

Even in the darkest of places and deepest of sins, Christ Jesus is there with open arms, loving you. Is this scary or encouraging to you? Why?

Heavenly Father, I thank you for loving me so perfectly that you sent your only Son to die on a cross for my salvation. I know that I am a broken sinner, yet I strive to serve and love others as our Savior and perfect example, Jesus Christ, served me. Thank you for your love.

—Kevin Streelman

How much time do we waste worrying about our needs in this world? I need to make that mortgage payment, I need to advance my career, I need that new car, I need to improve my golf game…our list of needs starts to look like our Christmas list. God tells us that he already knows what we need, and if we live for him first and foremost, he will give us all we ever need!

What do you really need right now in your life? More money, more status…or more trust, more hope, more love?

What is one thing you can do to "seek the Kingdom of God above all else, and live righteously" this week?

Heavenly Father, I trust in you. I acknowledge that the only true position I need is to be on my knees, trusting in your plan, your work, and your promise to provide whatever I need this beautiful day so long as I trust in you!

—Kevin Streelman

Scripture Reading: Joshua 1:9 NLT

This is my command—be strong and courageous! Do not be afraid or discouraged. For the LORD your God is with you wherever you go.

Joshua 1:9 happens to be Tom Lehman's life verse, something he shared with me a few years ago. Notice that God doesn't recommend or encourage Joshua to banish fear and doubt from his life—he commands it!

As others have said, courage is fear that has said its prayers. We will always have opportunities to fear. But we can choose whether to let that fear control us or to appropriate the Lord's strength in the face of fear.

Where in your life has fear dominated your thoughts and actions recently?

How can you keep yourself free from these burdens?

Lord, please grant me peace this beautiful day. Help me to rest, confident in the knowledge that fear need not rule my life on any playing field or anyplace in this world, for you are with me wherever I go, and I trust in the one and only true Savior, Jesus Christ!

—Kevin Streelman

Scripture Reading: Matthew 28:16-17

Then the eleven disciples went to Galilee, to the mountain where Jesus had told them to go. When they saw him, they worshiped him; but some doubted.

This is the first of four reflections on the Great Commission (Matthew 28:16-20).

In these first two verses, two things stand out. First, there were only 11 disciples, not 12. And second, some doubted.

Here is what I like about this passage—it encourages me because like the disciples, I often come up short and sometimes doubt. We might wonder, how was it possible for the disciples to see a risen Jesus and still doubt? But then again, are we any different? How is it possible for us to look back at centuries of God's faithfulness and still doubt?

Yet even in these shortcomings, Jesus prearranges a meeting. He has set you and me apart to work with him to fulfill the Great Commission.

What doubts have worked their way into your thoughts recently? What truths can you focus on to combat those doubts?

Where does Jesus want to send you to work with him and to fulfill the Great Commission? Are you willing to go?

Lord, help me today in my shortcomings and doubts. Please arrange to meet with me in a powerful way so your desires would also be mine.

—Ben Crane

Scripture Reading: Matthew 28:18

Then Jesus came to them and said, "All authority in heaven and on earth has been given to me."

quoted this verse incorrectly for years. I always thought the last two words were "to you." It makes sense, right? He is sending us out to change the world, so wouldn't he naturally give us the power? The answer is simply no. Jesus never relinquishes the power. He has all the authority in heaven and earth (that is a lot, by the way), and he keeps the power.

Where do your power, your gifts, your talents come from? From you? Think again...

Jesus has all authority—what does that mean for your life?

In what ways would you like to see Jesus's authority displayed in your life today?

Thank you, Lord, for coming to us. Come to me today in a powerful way, and help me to see your authority displayed in my life.

—Ben Crane

Scripture Reading: Matthew 28:19

Go and make disciples of all nations, baptizing them in the name of the Father and of the Son and of the Holy Spirit.

Dawson Trotman, founder of the Navigators, was so intent on making disciples that he founded the Fishermen's Club—a group of men whose object was to learn to win people to Christ through individual witness. Our call is to go and make disciples... all of us. How does this work for you? Could you spend some time thinking about one person whom you could help grow in his walk with Jesus?

I have been reading Francis Chan's book *Multiply* with two other players. It's about making disciples who make disciples. This has been a great source of encouragement to me even though my original intent was to encourage them.

What does making disciples mean to you?

Who is one person you can help grow in his or her faith?

Lord Jesus, by the power of your Holy Spirit, please lay on my heart one or two people whom you would like me to "do life" with so that we are making disciples who make disciples.

—Ben Crane

Scripture Reading: Matthew 28:20

...teaching them to obey everything I have commanded you. And surely I am with you always, to the very end of the age.

The Great Commission closes by reminding us of two things we need to know.

First, we need to know and obey Jesus's commands. This is always good for us to remember. What commandments do you think Jesus was referring to? Which one might you focus on today?

Second, we need to know that Jesus is with us every day, always, and to the end. He is with us on the first tee, and he is with us whether we win the tournament or miss the cut. He is with us, and he cares.

Is there someone you can encourage today by putting their needs in front of yours?

Is the thought of Jesus being with you "to the very end" comforting? Why or why not?

Lord, help me love someone else well today.

—Ben Crane

As Bob Dylan famously sang in 1979, "You've gotta serve somebody."

We are all slaves, right? But to whom? We can easily become slaves to the sinful greed of this world. We can become slaves of power, pleasure, or success. And of course, we can become enslaved through addiction.

Or we can choose to serve a different master—one who heals us and sets us free even as we serve him. Jesus served the Father in humble obedience. He lived in reverence and gave himself in sacrifice. As a result, the Father exalted Jesus and gave him all authority. As we humbly serve God, we can trust that he will raise us up in due time.

Who (or what) is your master? Maybe you have more than one. If someone were to shadow you for a week, who (or what) would he say is your master?

What brings you the deepest contentment?

Heavenly Father, help me to serve you today. I admit I look for contentment in various places. Help me to find my true contentment in you.

—Stewart Cink

46

Scripture Reading: Proverbs 27:19 NLT

As a face is reflected in water, so the heart reflects the real person.

Everything we say or do each day is a true projection of our heart. As the popular quote says, you are the only Bible some people will ever read.

The way we image God in our heart shapes the way others around us see God for themselves. This is one of the basic premises of our mission as followers of Christ. We have the opportunity for our lives not only to reflect Christ but also to magnify him.

Another famous quote, attributed to various people, encourages us, "Preach the gospel at all times. When necessary, use words."

What do people think of when they think of you?

How can you reflect Jesus Christ to others today?

Jesus, look deep into my heart today, and show me what is there. Do my actions glorify you? When they don't, help me to address the real problem—not just in my behavior, but in my heart.

—Stewart Cink

Scripture Reading: 1 Thessalonians 5:16-18

Rejoice always, pray continually, give thanks in all circumstances; for this is God's will for you in Christ Jesus.

Being thankful is easy when we've just played a great round, landed a huge promotion, or enjoyed a wonderful Thanksgiving turkey and dressing! But what if things aren't going so well? Does that mean God is any less great than in the good times?

We can give thanks to God for his greatness regardless of what we are experiencing. In fact, when our circumstances are difficult, we can be especially thankful that he is our source of strength, contentment, and peace. Troubles are opportunities for our faith to grow.

Are you usually more thankful for your circumstances or for God's grace?

How has God revealed his goodness to you recently?

God, I confess that my first response to difficult situations is not always to give you thanks. Renew my mind—help me to use every situation as an opportunity to give you thanks.

—Stewart Cink

Scripture Reading: Psalm 73:26

My flesh and my heart may fail, but God is the strength of my heart and my portion forever.

The psalmist is tormented by what he sees—godless pleasure seekers living in prosperity and ease.

Temptation was a real and tangible part of his life, just as it is in ours. Other people's fortunes can become a distraction and disrupt our focus on Jesus. The psalmist even goes so far as to question his own decision of faith—"Did I keep my heart pure for nothing? Did I keep myself innocent for no reason?" (verse 13 NLT).

If we don't deal with our bitterness, it will poison us. What's the cure? Turning our attention on God, the relationship he has established with us, and the wonderful inheritance he is preparing for us. These are true blessings, and they will last.

The psalmist finally understood when he "entered the sanctuary of God" (verse 17). How do you experience God's presence?

The psalmist learned to desire God above all else (verse 25). What do you desire most? Can you bring those desires to God?

Dear God, I repent of my jealousy, envy, and bitterness. I turn to you, and I thank you for being the strength of my heart and my portion forever.

—Stewart Cink

Scripture Reading: Hebrews 12:1 PHILLIPS

Surrounded then as we are by these serried ranks of witnesses, let us strip off everything that hinders us, as well as the sin which dogs our feet, and let us run the race that we have to run with patience.

Think about all the wonderful leaders who have influenced you. They may still be on this earth, but even if they aren't, their legacy is continuing to shape your life. They have inspired you to follow Christ. So whatever causes you any angst or hinders you in any way, strip it off. Start this day prayed up and clean.

The race you are running calls for endurance. Draw inspiration and encouragement from others' examples, and run the race God has for you with patience.

Name one person who has been an inspiration to your faith. How has this person impacted you?

What might be hindering you today? How can you strip it off?

Lord, I give you this day, this race I'm running, and all that happens in it. Thank you for providing me with inspiring examples and empowering me to run with patience.

—Ben Crane

Scripture Reading: Hebrews 12:3 PHILLIPS

Think constantly of him enduring all that sinful men could say against him and you will not lose your purpose or your courage.

What is the number one form of meditation—the mental activity that people do constantly? Worry!

We think about so many things and so many issues that are simply not our responsibility. The writer to the Hebrews encourages believers to think constantly of Jesus. Think of him enduring all that sinful men could say. Think of him loving. Think of him forgiving. Think of him trusting his Father even when he could not sense his presence.

By doing this, we keep our purpose and our courage strong!

How can you maintain your focus on Jesus today? How might that work in the middle of a busy day?

When you are feeling anxious, think about Pilippians 4:6-7 and give your worries to God?

Lord, I ask for a window into your purpose and your courage today. I give you this day. Help me to think constantly of you.

—Ben Crane

Scripture Reading: James 1:23-24

Anyone who listens to the word but does not do what it says is like someone who looks at his face in a mirror and, after looking at himself, goes away and immediately forgets what he looks like.

James tells us to not be like a man who looks at himself in the mirror but goes away and immediately forgets what he looks like.

I know I have done that many times. When reading the Bible or listening to someone give a message from the Word, my mind starts to wander. When all is done, I have no idea what I have read or heard. What an embarrassment! Listening, hearing, and understanding require commitment. This isn't always easy—it wasn't meant to be. The things we commit to, the things we focus our attention on, the things we repeatedly come back to…these are the things we allow to shape our lives.

Think of a time when you forgot something important—a name, an appointment, an anniversary or birthday. How did the experience make you feel?

What important, life-shaping truth can you focus on today?

Dear Father, I pray for a deep desire to look intently to you and into your Word today. Give me wisdom as I choose what I will focus on today.

—Tom Lehman

One of my core strategies in golf is to find what you do well and perfect it. For me, that is hitting a draw, and I have spent years and years working on that. It is not yet perfected, but it is a long way down the road from where I started.

But when it comes to my faith in God and my journey with him, the opposite is true. I can never perfect myself. Only the Author of my life, the Creator, can do that. He alone can empower us to be all he created us to be. The harder we try, the more dissatisfied we get. So instead, we need to let God take what he has done well (created us) and perfect it. And we do that by simply humbling ourselves before him and letting him work.

What might God be trying to perfect in your life recently? Where do you see him working?

How can you cooperate with God in this area? How can you make yourself more available to him?

Lord, I can't transform my life on my own. I want you to live your life through me. Work in my life to create a humble heart that will allow you to bring me to full maturity.

—Tom Lehman

Scripture Reading: Matthew 12:30 NLT

Anyone who isn't with me opposes me, and anyone who isn't working with me is actually working against me.

Sometimes everything in life seems to fall apart all at once. It might be at home, in your job, with your finances…it could be anything. We all have felt as if we were way, way under the pile with no clear way out.

That has happened to me on the golf course many times. Everything is just so far off that I don't know where to begin to fix it. Inevitably, I always go back to the basics, the fundamentals. Stance, posture, ball position…and then I always seem to be able to find my way back.

My walk with God is no different. Life's worries eventually lead to feeling totally alone with life spinning out of control. That's when I go back to the basics—to Jesus and his teaching that we are either with him or opposed to him. I never want to waste a day or even a moment by being against him. That foundational belief always brings me to my knees, seeking him.

How might you be opposing God's work in your life right now?

What does going back to the basics with God mean to you today?

Dear God, I seek your face today with all my heart. Let my life be an example of someone who is totally for you.

—Tom Lehman

Scripture Reading: Psalm 23:1-3

The LORD is my shepherd, I lack nothing. He makes me lie down in green pastures, he leads me beside quiet waters, he refreshes my soul.

One of the worst things I can do on a golf course is worry about a score or my place on the leaderboard before I even start the round. It is easy to do, however, and the by-product of such bad thinking is always fear and anxiety. It is just so easy to become consumed by the result rather than enjoying the moment-by-moment process of playing golf. It is so easy to get way ahead of myself.

God shows us a different way. Read Psalm 23. We see a man walking with God and God walking with him. Hope and courage, goodness and mercy come with the simple process of putting one foot in front of the other with God. Walking with God is a process, not a destination, and he is with us always. Joshua 1:9 (TLB) says, "Be bold and strong! Banish fear and doubt! For remember, the Lord your God is with you wherever you go."

What does "walking with God" mean to you?

What can you do to "enjoy the process with God" today?

Lord, slow me down. I want to walk with you through this life, not run ahead again. "Surely goodness and mercy will follow me all the days of my life, and I will dwell in the house of the LORD forever."

—Tom Lehman

Scripture Reading: John 15:7

If you remain in me and my words remain in you, ask whatever you wish, and it will be done for you.

Does this Scripture mean that you can have whatever you want? Is it a promise of prosperity?

No. It is a plea and a call to remain in Christ. "Remain" is said twice. "Remain in me." "My words remain in you." Keep these words in mind today. How can you remain in Christ as you go to work, care for your family, maintain your home, and so much more? The answer is simple...clear out the clutter. Sear this word into your memory and talk about it—"remain."

How do you remain in Jesus?

Have any particular words of Jesus remained in you this past week? Which ones?

Lord, help me to remain in you today as I fulfill the responsibilities you've given me.

—Stewart Cink

I have been crucified with Christ and I no longer live, but Christ lives in me. The life I now live in the body, I live by faith in the Son of God, who loved me and gave himself for me.

Have you had your funeral yet?

This Scripture says that you died with Christ and that you no longer live. You died with Christ…Christ is alive in you…you live by faith…what on earth do these statements even mean?

They mean that the old you is gone—the you that was separate from God and unable to restore your union with him. In Jesus's incarnation, God joined with humanity so humanity could be rejoined to God. Through your faith in Jesus, you can enjoy life with God!

What part of your life can you enjoy with God? All of it! Your marriage, your kids, your work, your friendships, your hobbies… God wants to walk with you in all of it!

Celebrate your funeral today—say goodbye forever to a life separated from God.

How can you enjoy walking in new life today—in relationship with God?

Lord, thank you for tearing down the barrier between humanity and you. Help me to walk by faith in you today!

—Stewart Cink

Scripture Reading: Hebrews 10:24-25

Let us consider how we may spur one another on toward love and good deeds, not giving up meeting together, as some are in the habit of doing, but encouraging one another—and all the more as you see the Day approaching.

This passage immediately reminds us of two life-changing truths.
First, we are not strong enough on our own to build a life that really makes a difference, a life filled with love and good deeds. Life is relentless, and our own resources are limited. Eventually, on our own, we'll be reduced to survival mode, just hanging on until the end.

Second, our relationships help us remain encouraged, vital, and strong. God has designed the Christian life to be lived in community. As we meet together, God opens his storehouse of provision, and through each other we receive power to love, to serve... to actually live in a way we never dreamed we could.

Whom can you encourage today? How could you build up that person today?

What encouraging thought or word can you share with friends today?

Lord, I give you this day and ask that you help me see ways to be an encouragement to others.

—Stewart Cink

Scripture Reading: John 5:24 NLT

I tell you the truth, those who listen to my message and believe in God who sent me have eternal life. They will never be condemned for their sins, but they have already passed from death into life.

Think of the first time you remember hearing from God, whether reading the Bible, hearing a sermon, or talking with another person. Think of the moment you asked Jesus into your life. Do you remember it? Do you realize the power of the moment that you responded to Jesus in your life? You crossed from death into life! Forever!

Who is the most recent convert to Christ you know? Whom do you hope will soon meet Christ and pass from death into life? Pray for these people.

When did you cross from death to life? Look for an opportunity to share your story with someone today.

What message from Jesus can you focus on today? Envision yourself walking with God through this day.

Lord, thank you for bringing me from death into life. Please help me receive your message and walk with you through faith today.

—Stewart Cink

Scripture Reading: Philippians 2:5-11 NLT

You must have the same attitude that Christ Jesus had. Though he was God, he did not think of equality with God as something to cling to. Instead, he gave up his divine privileges; he took the humble position of a slave and was born as a human being. When he appeared in human form, he humbled himself in obedience to God and died a criminal's death on a cross. Therefore God elevated him to the place of highest honor and gave him the name above all other names, that at the name of Jesus every knee should bow, in heaven and on earth and under the earth, and every tongue confess that Jesus Christ is Lord, to the glory of God the Father.

Jesus had every reason to be proud. He was there when everything was created—fish and birds and mammals of every size and description. Galaxies too big and too far away to even comprehend. Matter so small, it's like pure energy. Mountains and rivers and deserts and forests...the wonder of creation boggles the mind.

I like to brag about stuff, like my Ping-Pong skills. But the Son of God was born in a barn, rode into Jerusalem on a donkey, washed his disciples' feet, and gave his life on a cross as if he were a common criminal. God is humble. I am not. I want to be, but I'm not. Sometimes I think I'm starting to become humble...but then I want to brag about it!

What amazes you the most about God and his creation? Spend a moment to praise him for his jaw-dropping works.

Consider memorizing this passage as a step toward adopting Christ's attitude of humility.

Jesus, my pride looks so silly in the light of your humble life and sacrifice. Please help me love as you love and serve as you serve today.

—Ben Crane

Scripture Reading: 1 John 4:18-19

There is no fear in love. But perfect love drives out fear, because fear has to do with punishment. The one who fears is not made perfect in love. We love because he first loved us.

We underestimate the power of love. When the love of Christ captures our hearts, we need nothing else to satisfy us. Through our faith in him, we are more than conquerors. Trusting Jesus allows us to overcome stress, anxiety, and fear.

On a Sunday morning before the final round of the 2011 McGladrey Classic, Joel Stock (my caddie) and I met 2 hours and 20 minutes before our tee time to do our devotional, just as we always do. The devotion for the day was prepared by our friend Neil on this verse. It's amazing to me that when we focus on Christ's love, there is no room in us for fear. It has been cast out by our faith.

I struggle so frequently on the golf course with fear. Fear of not making the cut, fear of not measuring up, fear of not doing my best. During the round Joel and I kept claiming to each other that God's perfect love cast out all fear, and we moved to a place of freedom and joy and trust. Thank you, Lord, that this is who we are in you.

Confess your greatest fear to the Lord and to someone you trust.

Do you believe that God's plan for your life is better than what you are afraid of?

Heavenly Father, thank you that you are love and that you love me in spite of my fear and disbelief. Help me to release to you this burden of fear and to rejoice in your love.

—Ben Crane

Scripture Reading: Ephesians 3:20-21

Now to him who is able to do immeasurably more than all we ask or imagine, according to his power that is at work within us, to him be glory in the church and in Christ Jesus throughout all generations, for ever and ever! Amen.

A good friend introduced me to these verses during my rookie season. They have since become two of my "life verses"— favorite inspirational passages that continue to apply to our lives.

Looking back over the past 13 years on the tour, I can clearly see that when I pursue God's will, he always shows up! Whether I am speaking at an outreach, putting on a golf tournament fund-raiser, trying to encourage others, leading a Bible study, or following him out of my comfort zone in other ways, God does things that are immeasurably better than I could have imagined. When I go to play in a tournament, I often pray, "Lord, make up the difference today." I have witnessed him answering this prayer many, many times!

I know how hard it can be to step out and put yourself in a situation that tests your faith. But I also know that when we live out our faith, when we function as salt and light in the world, we give God the opportunity to do something great in and through us.

Is God leading you out of your comfort zone? How might he have you demonstrate your faith today?

How has God blessed you recently beyond what you expected?

Heavenly Father, help me to follow you out of my comfort zone today.

—Ben Crane

Scripture Reading: 2 Corinthians 12:7

In order to keep me from becoming conceited, I was given a thorn in my flesh, a messenger of Satan, to torment me. Three times I pleaded with the Lord to take it away from me. But he said to me, "My grace is sufficient for you, for my power is made perfect in weakness."

To carry a thorn around can be such a burden. But I have learned it can also produce a humility that we would lack otherwise. Larry Moody, our chaplain on the tour, has taught us that our number one goal in life should be to depend on God. Humility produces dependence.

My wife, Heather, helped facilitate a ladies' Bible study for inmates in the Dallas county jail. The women took turns sharing their "thorns." The stories were heartbreaking, but Heather said she had never sensed such humility. The women shared a desperate desire for God to rescue, redeem, and restore their broken lives. Isn't that what we want—a deep humility to let God use our brokenness and do something great in and through us? Rather than always praying that God would change our circumstances as soon as possible, let's accept situations that humble us so we can learn to depend on God.

Do you struggle with a thorn in your life? What is your thorn?

How does God show you that through your weakness you can better serve him?

Lord, I pray that this thorn in my flesh, like Paul's, would be used for your glory.

—Ben Crane

Scripture Reading: Philippians 1:12-14

Now I want you to know, brothers and sisters, that what has happened to me has actually served to advance the gospel. As a result, it has become clear throughout the whole palace guard and to everyone else that I am in chains for Christ. And because of my chains, most of the brothers and sisters have become confident in the Lord and dare all the more to proclaim the gospel without fear.

You probably haven't been in jail recently. (I hope you won't be!) Paul was imprisoned through no fault of his own, but he didn't pout, he didn't get angry, and he didn't ask for pity. Instead, he accepted his difficult circumstances, maintained his commitment, and focused on his process. Paul continued to advance the gospel because the gospel is unstoppable!

Other people evidently looked in on Paul's difficulties, perhaps to see how he was faring. They were inspired to see Paul stick to his course regardless of his circumstances.

What goal can you focus on today regardless of the circumstances? What do you want the day to bring about?

Have you ever felt imprisoned by difficult circumstances? What happens when you take your eyes off the goal?

Lord, I give you this day. Help me to advance the gospel in every situation and to remain confident and joyful in you as you work in and through me.

—Cameron Tringale

Scripture Reading: Titus 1:7-8

Since an overseer manages God's household, he must be blameless—not overbearing, not quick-tempered, not given to drunkenness, not violent, not pursuing dishonest gain. Rather, he must be hospitable, one who loves what is good, who is self-controlled, upright, holy and disciplined.

When a house is built, the owner and the builder walk through together one last time and make a "punch list"—a final list of items that need to get done. I love Titus for this very reason—he gives us a punch list.

You are a leader. We all are leaders at some point each day. Hear the words—blameless, not overbearing or quick-tempered, not drunk or violent or dishonest, hospitable, loving what is good, controlled, upright, holy, and disciplined. What a challenge to think about all these areas of our lives! God has tough qualifications, doesn't he? What a responsibility! But God gives us the power we need to live out these qualities in our leadership positions.

What word on this punch list would you like to focus on today? Why?

In what areas might God be calling you to be a leader?

Lord, please lead me today as I lead others to you.

—Cameron Tringale

Scripture Reading: 2 Timothy 2:15

Do your best to present yourself to God as one approved, a worker who does not need to be ashamed and who correctly handles the word of truth.

I like to use the phrase "at the end of the day." I use it to summarize the direction we are going and identify what we want to have accomplished.

This verse is a goal for all of us regardless of our profession, our skills, our age, or anything else that makes us unique. We all are striving to be people who are approved by God and who handle his Word correctly. How have the past few weeks gone for you in this regard? This verse provides a great "end of the day" goal for us!

How have you been "presenting" yourself to God lately? Are you giving him your very best? What in this verse is God whispering to you about?

At the end of this day, what do you want to have accomplished? What do you want others to see in your life?

Lord, I pray that today, at the end, I will have given you my all.

—Cameron Tringale

Scripture Reading: Mark 13:10

And the gospel must first be preached to all nations.

Jesus was always reminding his disciples of three things—a clear vision, an inspiring mission, and a refusal to accept false boundaries.

We can quickly forget our vision—what are we about? Where do we want to go? What do we want our lives to look like? How about mission—why do you do what you do? What is your bottom-line motivation that keeps you working, hoping, and believing? Regarding boundaries, we can be quick to place limits, walls, and definitions where God has not set them.

Christ wants to widen all three—our vision, our mission, and our boundaries. Today, think bigger. Remind yourself that Jesus is the author of any BHAG (big, hairy, audacious goal) we could have—his is the salvation of the world!

In what ways have you sensed your vision blurring, your boundaries closing in, or your mission being watered down?

In a few paragraphs, write out a statement of your life's mission and vision.

Lord, please help me think clearly and expansively today.

—Cameron Tringale

God made him who had no sin to be sin for us, so that in him we might become the righteousness of God.

This is the bare-bones foundation of Christianity. Jesus walked on this earth and faced every temptation we do, and yet he never sinned. Jesus then took on all of our sins as if he had committed them and died on the cross, acting as our substitute.

If your friend got a speeding ticket, would you be willing to take his place and face all the consequences—the court time, the fines, and the increased insurance premiums? What if your friend committed a crime that sentenced him to jail? Would you be willing to serve his prison sentence for him? Jesus took our place because he loves us unconditionally. His death and resurrection wiped the slate clean and made us pure.

We are justified by faith in Jesus's death and resurrection. Look at the word "justified" and think of it as "just as if" we had never sinned.

God became like us so that we might become like him. How might God be making you more like him today?

What sin would you like to trade in for God's righteousness today?

Lord, thank you for leading a perfect life on earth, dying for my sins, and rising again so I can enjoy new life with you now and forever.

—Mark Wilson

Scripture Reading: Acts 14:19-21

Some Jews came from Antioch and Iconium and won the crowd over. They stoned Paul and dragged him outside the city, thinking he was dead. But after the disciples had gathered around him, he got up and went back into the city. The next day he and Barnabas left for Derbe. They preached the good news in that city and won a large number of disciples.

If you were beaten so badly that people dragged you out of town and left you for dead, would you get up and go right back into the city? Then would you go to another city and preach the same news that got you beat up in the first place? I believe wholeheartedly that Jesus Christ is alive and that his death on the cross saves me from all of my sins, but I have never been beaten for that belief. So I wonder…if I were confronted, would I stand my ground?

I enjoy my life. I play golf for a living. I have a loving family, and I enjoy God's creation in many ways. But life is even better when we submit completely to God, and it will become better still when we live with God for eternity. We can cling to that truth when our faith is tested.

Have you had the privilege of suffering (perhaps emotionally or socially) for the sake of the gospel?

Paul was a man on a mission. Do you have a life mission that empowers you to overcome obstacles?

Dear God, please help me clarify my life's mission, and give me strength to continue in the face of opposition.

—Mark Wilson

A few years ago, in the final round of the Humana Challenge, a tournament of low scoring, I started the day with a three-shot lead but was one over par through ten holes. I was sure I'd lost my lead, but I finished with four birdies on the back to win.

A lot of people asked me why I hung in there. My thinking all day was that a round of golf is eighteen holes. Some days start with birdies, others end with birdies, and sadly, some days include no birdies. With eight holes left, I had plenty of opportunities to get back under par. Besides, the golf season was just beginning, and if the birdies didn't come at all that day and I finished back in the pack, I had an entire year left for some good play to occur.

In a word, I was patient. If only my thinking was this clear all the time!

Contrast that with impatience, which leads to quick decisions that are often regrettable. When I am calm and patient with my quarreling sons, I can find a good solution. However, when I let impatience get the best of me, I'm likely to make a quick, foolish decision.

Recall a quick decision that you lived to regret. Now recall a time when patience led to a better response.

What situation in your life is calling for patience today?

Lord, fill me today so that I may exhibit the fruit of the Spirit, including patience.

—Mark Wilson

Scripture Reading: Philippians 4:11-12

I am not saying this because I am in need, for I have learned to be content whatever the circumstances. I know what it is to be in need, and I know what it is to have plenty. I have learned the secret of being content in any and every situation, whether well fed or hungry, whether living in plenty or in want.

Contentment is often elusive. How do we ever get it? Has anybody actually found it? Golf, a sport of statistics and rankings, seems to set us up for discontentment. Aren't you always trying to do better? Hit the ball farther? Shave off one more stroke?

> America is a social experiment founded on the pursuit of happiness…Money, materialism, sex, romance, religion, family, and fame are all pursuits of the same human craving—joy. But apart from Jesus, we never get there. In an odd twist of fate, America, for all her life and liberty, is one of the most depressed nations in the world. And many of us are mad at God.[1]

Three things rob us of contentment: jealousy, stress, and comparison. However, thankfulness can cure us of all of these. All of life is grace; all of life is a gift. Everything is a gift from God. We are blessed, and we can be content.

What is currently robbing you of joy? Bitterness? Stress? Cast these burdens on God today.

List five wonderful gifts from God to you. Think of them often today.

Lord, thank you for loving me and establishing a relationship with me. You are more than enough for me.

—Ben Crane

[1] John Mark Comer, *My Name Is Hope* (Jakarta: Graphe, 2012), 106.

Scripture Reading: Romans 9:33 MSG

Careful! I've put a huge stone on the road to Mount Zion, a stone you can't get around. But the stone is me! If you're looking for me, you'll find me on the way, not in the way.

Sometimes God doesn't fit into our plans.

Many of the religious people of Jesus's day had the same problem. When God became a man, many people stumbled over him because he didn't fit their preconceived idea of what the Messiah should be like. He didn't promote their agenda.

When we make our plans and set our course apart from God, he graciously plants himself in our way so we'll stumble over him and reconsider our trajectory. Even better, when we determine to follow him from the outset and keep our eyes peeled for him along the way, we will find him.

Are you in any difficult situations? Instead of asking, "How can I get out of this?" try asking, "What is God teaching me?"

Think about a challenge you've experienced. Did God bring anything good out of that situation?

Father, when I face adversity and pain, help me to consider whether I'm headed my own way and bumping up against you. Help me to find you along the way, and equip me to reach out to others and encourage them.

—Ben Crane

Scripture Reading: Isaiah 41:10

So do not fear, for I am with you; do not be dismayed, for I am your God. I will strengthen you and help you; I will uphold you with my righteous right hand.

Here God tells the Israelites not to fear, not to be dismayed, for he will lift them up and protect them from anything coming their way. What an awesome, loving God! The Scriptures repeatedly single out fear as a worthless, worldly concern that God simply has no time for. He doesn't *recommend* that we let go of our earthly fears—he *commands* us to!

What did you wake up worrying about this morning? Ask God to ease your burden.

Clarify exactly what it is you are afraid might happen. Ask, "So, what if that does happen?" with each potentially negative outcome. Compare your answer with today's verse.

Lord and Father, I trust in your strength and your plan, not mine. Even though I am weak and imperfect, you have my back. I thank you for that, and I love you for that. Help me today to trust in you, to let go of my earthly worries and fears, and to set my sights on your eternal kingdom!

—Kevin Streelman

Scripture Reading: Mark 10:14-15 NLT

When Jesus saw what was happening, he was angry with his disciples. He said to them, "Let the children come to me. Don't stop them! For the Kingdom of God belongs to those who are like these children. I tell you the truth, anyone who doesn't receive the Kingdom of God like a child will never enter it."

To enter God's kingdom by faith, we must become like children—helpless, unable to provide for ourselves, and completely dependent on God's mercy and grace.

As most of us become adults, we may remember how good children have got it. They find joy in almost everything, they haven't been jaded by this broken world, they are completely honest in their thoughts and actions, and they know that those who love them will care for them. That is what our Lord wants of us—to depend totally on him, share completely in his love, and enjoy life with him. So approach your day with a childlike, joyful, and humble outlook, a serving attitude, and a soul that depends on him.

How can you become more childlike and depend on God more?

How can you serve as an example so that others may notice these changes and pursue them?

Lord, please help me to recognize the childlike behaviors I have lost and to develop them again in my relationship with you. I know that you are in control of my life, and I pray that my dependence on you will be unwavering and complete.

—Kevin Streelman

Scripture Reading: Philippians 1:21-24

For to me, to live is Christ and to die is gain. If I am to go on living in the body, this will mean fruitful labor for me. Yet what shall I choose? I do not know! I am torn between the two: I desire to depart and be with Christ, which is better by far; but it is more necessary for you that I remain in the body.

Most of us know the feeling of hitting the sweet spot on a golf club, but do we know the feeling of finding the sweet spot in life? Paul did. Sitting in a Roman jail, he is having an honest conversation with himself, admitting that it would be so much better to let go of this world and go spend eternity with the Lord. But he catches himself and says, "No, not yet. I have a job here, a very important job, and for now I'm going to trust in God's plan." When it came to fulfilling his purpose in the world, Paul was all in. Are we?

What am I making too important on this earth today?

What am I not giving enough importance to today?

Heavenly Father, please help me today to quit worrying about status and money. They hold no significance. You are my significance. I believe in your life and the resurrection and the incredible world to come. For yours is the kingdom and the power and the glory forever! Amen!

—Kevin Streelman

On Jesus's last night with his disciples, after washing their feet and predicting Judas's betrayal and Peter's denial, Jesus gave his friends some final instructions: "Listen, this is important. It is imperative that you love one another, just as I have loved you— unconditionally." If this is one of the last things Jesus says to his disciples, it must be something we need to take very seriously.

Love heals, love transcends, love forgives, and love represents our faith in Jesus, who came here to sacrifice everything so we could have everything.

Whom can you show love to today—someone you wouldn't normally think of serving?

What prohibits you from following Jesus's example of forgiving and loving others?

Lord, please show me someone today who needs to be shown love. Please give me the opportunity to demonstrate your grace through my love for another person this day. Help me represent your kingdom today through some simple acts of kindness and love. Thank you for first showing that love to me.

—Kevin Streelman

Scripture Reading: Romans 15:7 MSG

So reach out and welcome one another to God's glory. Jesus did it; now you do it! Jesus, staying true to God's purposes, reached out in a special way.

Polite people know how to put you at ease. Their words and actions send a consistent message: "You're welcome here!"

We say, "You're welcome" when we're happy to serve someone or to give someone a gift. We also say "welcome" when we greet people. We show that we are thankful for people, grateful for their places in our lives, and appreciative of what they have done for us. Of course, the greatest "You're welcome" and the greatest "Welcome" were given to us by Jesus. He has served us and given us the greatest of gifts, and now he welcomes us into a loving relationship with God.

Who taught you how to be polite? How has this skill served you?

What are you grateful for today?

Lord, please help me see all the opportunities you have placed before me to serve others joyfully, give to them freely, and welcome them warmly today.

—Bubba Watson

Scripture Reading: Philippians 3:13-14

Brothers and sisters, I do not consider myself yet to have taken hold of it. But one thing I do: Forgetting what is behind and straining toward what is ahead, I press on toward the goal to win the prize for which God has called me heavenward in Christ Jesus.

Forgetting the past isn't easy. It's hard to walk to the next tee box and not think about the bogey (or worse) on the previous hole. But God wants us to put troubles behind us, to look forward, and to press on for what lies ahead. As believers in Christ, we are always going to have our daily losses. We certainly want to learn from these moments, but we need to keep our eyes on the prize, which is found in Jesus. Our goal is to "press on," to be "straining toward what is ahead." I can honestly say that this has been my experience—forgetting what is behind and moving on for the prize.

What do you need to leave behind today?

What steps can you take to trust Christ with these "losses" (James 1:2) and move toward the prize?

Lord, help me to forget the losses and to strive toward the true prize, which is found in you.

—Bubba Watson

Scripture Reading: Philippians 2:2 NLT

Make me truly happy by agreeing wholeheartedly with each other, loving one another, and working together with one mind and purpose.

One of the impressive aspects of the Masters at Augusta National is the crowd control. I'm amazed that people actually agree to the culture of Augusta—no cell phones, no autographs outside of designated areas, no litter, and no running. The most impressive is that people work together, sharing their seats in a way that is unlike any PGA tournament I am aware of. People seem to care for other patrons and even look out for each other.

I love this passage of Scripture because it gives me great hope. We are all on the same team—we're all created by God. All of us have the same mind and purpose, but sometimes we need to be reminded. It's not about a green jacket—it's about loving God with my whole heart and loving those whom God puts around me.

Who has God placed on your own team?

How can you treat others in ways that demonstrate that we are all on the same team?

Lord, help me remember today that we are on the same team, and please remind me of our heavenly goals.

—Bubba Watson

Scripture Reading: 1 John 3:13 NLT

So don't be surprised, dear brothers and sisters, if the world hates you.

What is the apostle John referring to as "the world"?
It is the pursuit of all things that in the end pass away. It includes the things man values but God doesn't. The world doesn't love what God loves, and the world doesn't do things the way God does.

I experienced this contrast in a tournament when my last putt rattled to the bottom of the hole, securing my win. That moment was a showcase of God's love and purposes. In what other sport will your competitors actually make their way out to celebrate with you? In this moment, God's kingdom showed how it exists in such contrast to the world.

Where do you see the world sneaking into your life, enticing you to follow its ways?

Where have you seen God's love showcased in a way that contrasted sharply with the world's ways?

Lord, I give you this day, I give you my heart, and I ask you to showcase your love against the world's backdrop.

—Bubba Watson

Scripture Reading: Colossians 4:2

Devote yourselves to prayer, being watchful and thankful.

A few years ago, a friend's son was critically injured. In addition to giving the boy excellent care, the EMTs, doctors, nurses, friends, and family all prayed for him—and his recovery has been miraculous!

If we want see God's power displayed, we do well to devote ourselves to prayer. We can always be on the lookout for opportunities to invite God into difficult situations. And as we pray, we can thank him in advance for always hearing us.

Whom or what can you add to your prayer list today?

What answered prayer can you thank God for today (regardless of whether the outcome was what you wanted)?

Father, thank you for answering all our prayers and for the miracles you perform every day!

—Davis Love III

Scripture Reading: 1 John 5:5

Who is it that overcomes the world? Only the one who believes that Jesus is the Son of God.

J.B. Phillips famously translated Romans 12:2 this way: "Don't let the world around you squeeze you into its own mould, but let God re-mould your minds from within." What does the world's mould include? An anti-god worldview. Performance-based relationships. Self-centered desires. Shame, fear, and anger.

The kingdom of God is just the opposite. God is everywhere. Everyone is worthy of unconditional love. Service is the path to true fulfillment. We are free from shame, delivered from fear, and released from controlling anger.

What's the key to experiencing the kingdom of God right here in our crazy world? Believing in Jesus!

Have you felt squeezed into the world's mold? In what way?

Why might believing be the key to overcoming?

Lord, help me to cling to you every day and reject the false idols the world offers.

—Davis Love III

Scripture Reading: 2 Corinthians 1:21-22

He anointed us, set his seal of ownership on us, and put his Spirit in our hearts as a deposit, guaranteeing what is to come.

This verse always gives me a feeling of peace. God chose me!

Think of the times you've been chosen—as a player on a team, as an employee, as a friend, as a spouse…How did those experiences make you feel—Recognized? Important? Loved?

The most important thing about you, the very center of your identity, is this—the God of all creation has chosen you. And this wasn't just a one-time thing. His Spirit lives in you every day, a deposit of the even greater things to come.

How does *that* make you feel!

Do you feel confident that you belong to God? Read today's verse slowly and out loud. Make it personal: "He anointed *me*, set his seal of ownership on *me*…"

Do your shortcomings negate God's choice?

Eternal God, thank you for guaranteeing our place in eternity with you by placing your Holy Spirit in us. Help us to truly know that we are free from having to work our way into your favor. By faith and nothing else, we have been given your presence, now and forever.

—Davis Love III

Scripture Reading: Revelation 12:7-9

War broke out in heaven. Michael and his angels fought against the dragon, and the dragon and his angels fought back. But he was not strong enough, and they lost their place in heaven. The great dragon was hurled down—that ancient serpent called the devil, or Satan, who leads the whole world astray. He was hurled to the earth, and his angels with him.

What a wonderful picture of heaven's victory over hell! But notice what is happening now—Satan is leading the whole world astray. We have to be strong and fight back!

We can be completely confident because God, who is in us, is greater than Satan, who is in the world (1 John 4:4). But that doesn't mean we can be complacent. We must be careful not to be led astray (2 Corinthians 11:3). And we dare not allow the god of this world to continue blinding people's minds (2 Corinthians 4).

God has defeated the enemy. We are privileged to enforce God's victory!

In what ways might Satan try to lead you astray?

What methods can you use to resist Satan's influence in your life?

Father God, thank you for protecting me from these dark forces. Give me wisdom to recognize enemy attacks.

—Davis Love III

Scripture Reading: Mark 4:23 NLT

Anyone with ears to hear should listen and understand.

God created us in his own image (Genesis 1:27). He designed us as relational beings with a desire to communicate and with ears so we could hear.

Everybody has ears, but not everyone hears, listens, and understands in the way Jesus is describing. In fact, Jesus taught in parables to reveal truth to those whose hearts were open and to disguise the truth from those who were too prejudiced or stubborn to hear what he was saying. We're not likely to hear God speak directly to us in an audible voice, but thankfully the Gospels are filled with Jesus's words and his message to the world. To listen to Jesus's words is as easy as reading the Scriptures. The Holy Spirit helps us understand and interpret God's Word in the depths of our hearts. To truly hear Jesus's words, we must believe them, use them in conversations, and let them shape our attitudes.

When I was a child, my parents used to say to me, "Cameron, did you hear me? Are you listening?" Their words would go in one ear and out the other. I hope that never happens when God speaks to me!

We tend to hear God's voice more when we're in the habit of obeying him. How will you demonstrate your obedience today?

What might dull your spiritual sense of hearing? What might sharpen it?

Dear Lord, thank you for the gift of being able to hear you speak in your Word.

—Cameron Tringale

Someone much wiser than me once told me that there are three elements to growing your relationship with Jesus: prayer, fellowship with other believers, and spending time in God's Word.

If you have kids or younger siblings, you probably relate to today's verse easily. When my younger sister was born, she relied completely on everyone else to take care of her—change her diapers, get her dressed, entertain her, feed her, and on and on. God wants his followers to have this kind of reliance on his Word. He wants us to feast on it for our nourishment and to feel hungry and discontent when it is absent from our lives. Just as babies need milk to grow up into healthy, functioning adults, we need a steady diet of time in the Bible to grow as Christians.

How might you cultivate a longing for the pure spiritual milk? List a few realistic steps you can take.

Are you growing up into salvation? What might that look like in your life?

Dear Lord, thank you for preserving your Word and making it available to me today. Help me to drink from your Word the way an infant drinks from its bottle. Only you have what I need, so help me develop my appetite for you.

—Cameron Tringale

Scripture Reading: 2 Corinthians 3:15-16

A veil lies over their hearts. But when one turns to the Lord, the veil is removed.

Have you ever spoken with someone, only to realize that they didn't have a clue what you were talking about? That's what happens when unbelievers try to understand spiritual truth. A veil of misunderstanding covers their hearts. They just don't get it—until they turn to the Lord. When we turn to the Lord, we change our direction away from this fallen world and toward a life of knowing and pursuing the Son of God.

The New Testament pictures the church as the bride of Christ (Ephesians 5:25-27,32; Revelation 19:7-9; 21:2,9). Just as a groom beams with anticipation as the wedding procession begins, so Jesus eagerly waits to embrace us. And when he draws us to himself, giving us the faith to boldly accept his invitation, he lifts the veil of our own sin and rebellion from our eyes so we can see his glory and with transformed minds begin to pursue him with our lives.

Take a moment to reflect back to the time you first turned toward Jesus and your veil was lifted. Then consider your spiritual posture today. Are you still facing the Lord? If not, why? Have you put back on any veils of sin and selfishness?

Ask Jesus to remove the veil from the eyes and heart of someone you know.

Heavenly Father, thank you for your Son. Thank you for pursuing me and inviting me to know you intimately. Help me to turn to you today.

—Cameron Tringale

Scripture Reading: Nehemiah 6:3 ESV

I sent messengers to them, saying, "I am doing a great work and I cannot come down. Why should the work stop while I leave it and come down to you?"

Work and distractions. Almost on a daily basis, professional golfers can expect reps, caddies, fans, and the media to turn our focus away from our work. We learn how to navigate the various diversions so we can pursue our best golf game, but what about pursuing Jesus in our everyday lives?

As Christians, our "great work" is living out the gospel and spreading the good news, but staying on task isn't always easy. Culture encourages us to focus on work, wealth, possessions… and our favorite sports teams. How cautious are we of the influences in our lives—books and magazines, TV shows, radio programs, music, and people we meet? None of these things are bad, but sometimes they can divert us from serving God. We are free to enjoy the many offerings of our culture and this world, but we must prioritize a relationship with and service to our Lord in our schedules and in our hearts.

What is likely to distract you from your great work of following Christ?

What can help you stay on track in your great work?

Dear Lord, today and always, help me to be as committed as Nehemiah when it comes to doing your great work.

—Cameron Tringale

Scripture Reading: 2 Corinthians 12:9

But [God] said to me, "My grace is sufficient for you, for my power is made perfect in weakness." Therefore I will boast all the more gladly of my weakness, so that the power of Christ may rest upon me.

I meditated on this verse during the Wells Fargo Championship and the US Open. Playing with Tiger the first two rounds was nerve-racking to say the least, considering I was on my home course in my hometown. Just being in a major creates pressure. As I meditated on this verse all week, it finally hit me in the fairway of number eleven on Sunday that God's grace is in fact enough for us. The grace he showed in Jesus's death and resurrection for our benefit was more than enough. I felt weak at the US Open on the back nine Sunday, but his power was being made perfect in my weakness. We need to rely on God daily for his strength and power.

What weakness do you have that can help you rely on Christ's power?

In what way is God's grace sufficient for you?

Lord, give me courage to confess my sins and my need for you. I want to rely on you today and not on myself. Help me, Lord, to revel in your grace.

—Webb Simpson

Scripture Reading: Psalm 103:10-12

He does not deal with us according to our sins, nor repay us according to our iniquities. For as high as the heavens are above the earth, so great is his steadfast love toward those who fear him; as far as the east is from the west, so far does he remove our transgressions from us.

Aren't you glad God doesn't give us what we deserve?

We can agree that if God in fact did repay us according to our sins, we would be in a horrible predicament. We all fall short of God's standard, which is perfection. Therefore we all deserve the most severe penalty. But we who fear him—who believe, love, and stand in awe of him—have learned that God in his faithfulness and love looks over our sin and removes our wickedness from us. And this has all been made possible by Jesus's death on the cross at Calvary. This is good news!

When a young child makes a mistake, do his mother and father love him any less? Confess one of your shortcomings to God and envision his gracious response.

Think of a person who has wronged you. Can you remove his or her transgressions from your relationship?

Heavenly Father, you are too good and kind to me. I want to accept your free grace daily. Thank you, Lord, for not dealing with me according to my sins and iniquities. Thank you for your steadfast love and faithfulness.

—Webb Simpson

What do we have to do in order to receive the gospel, or good news?

Nothing. All we can do is believe—believe that the good news is true. What is the good news? It is that we can live eternally with God. How, by doing something? No, by believing that Jesus is who he claims to be—the perfect Son of God. He bore the wrath of our just Father, who wants atonement for all the sins of the world, including our failures, shortcomings, mistakes, and sins. The Son of God took our place on the cross, where justice was served. If we believe in him, then we are hidden with him. We are given eternity with God the Father because of the eternal Son of God. We didn't do anything to receive this free gift of grace. We just believed.

Why then do we feel as if we need to do something after we believe? Because he's done so much for us, we want to do something for him. But if that happens, it becomes about me again. Oh, the narcissism! It's not about me—it's about him and what he's done. So we live in this freedom of not having to do anything in order to prove our worth. What marvelous, beautiful, sacrificial, freeing grace!

What have you believed you had to do to be saved?

Though we can't earn God's grace, we can humbly express our appreciation for it. How can you express your thankfulness to God for his grace today?

God, I do believe! I confess that I am free from having to earn my salvation, free from having to perform to establish my value. Thank you for your wonderful grace!

—Webb Simpson

Scripture Reading: John 1:3-4,40-42 ESV

All things were made through him, and without him was not anything made that was made. In him was life, and the life was the light of men...One of the two who heard John speak and followed Jesus was Andrew, Simon Peter's brother. He first found his own brother Simon and said to him, "We have found the Messiah" (which means Christ). He brought him to Jesus. Jesus looked at him and said, "You are Simon the son of John. You shall be called Cephas" (which means Peter).

Andrew brings his brother Simon to Jesus. Jesus singles out Simon and renames him Peter, which means "rock."

Was Andrew jealous? Did he wonder why Jesus didn't give him a new name? What did Peter have that Andrew didn't? Verse 3 says of Jesus, "All things were made through him"—including Peter and Andrew. God created each of them for their own unique purpose. Maybe Andrew's purpose was to bring other people to Jesus just as he brought his brother Peter.

The Bible is the living, truthful Word of God, so verse 3 must apply to us as well—Jesus made each of us. He knows what's inside us and has a purpose for each of us. We are important to him.

Do you have a sense of God's unique purpose for you? Write down some possible aspects of it.

Think of someone who has a clear sense of purpose. Thank God for that person and for giving him or her a unique assignment.

God, you lovingly created me for a purpose. I dedicate myself to you, excited to see what you have in store for me.

—Webb Simpson

Scripture Reading: Micah 6:8 MSG

He's already made it plain how to live, what to do, what God is looking for in men and women. It's quite simple: Do what is fair and just to your neighbor, be compassionate and loyal in your love, and don't take yourself too seriously—take God seriously.

My pastor came to me after a service and suggested I think about this verse throughout the year. The idea was simple—to have a verse to live by on and off the course. The end of the verse is my favorite part. The moment we step in front of God and his plans for us, that's the moment our own agenda has become too important.

How can you make sure you're taking God's will more seriously than your own?

How can you demonstrate compassion and loyalty to someone today?

Lord, help me to walk in faith each day, trusting in your will for my life. My thoughts, agenda, goals...may they all fall in place behind you. Thank you for the beautiful life you have given me.

—Scott Stallings

Scripture Reading: Proverbs 22:6

Start children off on the way they should go, and even when they are old they will not turn from it.

I'm gonna be a dad!

That excites me more than I can say, but it also completely terrifies me. I don't know this son of mine yet, but I already want the world for him. The thing is, what I want doesn't really matter. The Lord's will for his life is already taken care of. My wife and I have to check our own plans for him at the door and walk in faith daily, trusting that he's in the Lord's hands.

What are you holding too tightly? Entrust it to the Lord today.

List a few of your roles. Are you a father, a son, a husband, a worker? In each role, briefly describe "the way [you] should go."

Lord, not my will be done, but yours—that's my prayer. Help me to exercise an appropriate amount of control in every situation. And when worry and stress grow in me, help me to release even more to you.

—Scott Stallings

Scripture Reading: James 1:17 ESV

Every good gift and every perfect gift is from above, coming down from the Father of lights with whom there is no variation or shadow due to change.

My wife and I are about to have a drastic change in our lives—a child! Until now, we have based our decisions solely on ourselves. Now the time has come for all of that to change, and that can be overwhelming.

Change can be a good thing, and it will give us a chance to grow. This new life is one of God's good and perfect gifts to us and not something to be feared.

Best of all, though our circumstances will change, God never changes. We can always depend on him to be utterly faithful.

What changes in your life are on the horizon? How do they make you feel? Entrust them to God today.

How can God's unchanging nature help you navigate change in your life?

Lord, thank you for change. No, I really mean it! Even when I hate it and try to run as far from it as I can, it ends up being good for me. Thank you for loving me so much that even as fast as I try to run, all I have to do is turn around, and you will be right there waiting for me with open arms. Help me to see change as a gift from you.

—Scott Stallings

How do we do everything for the glory of God?

I play golf professionally. God has given me the skills I need to be good at it, and it's what I've wanted to do since the seventh grade. In order to use this gift to the fullest and show God my gratitude, I work hard at it. I strive to be disciplined, positive, and process oriented. I try to set high goals, trust God with the results, and see where he takes me. This brings him glory!

When we believe and trust in Jesus, God gives us the amazing gift of eternal life. In light of this we can bring him glory regardless of our circumstances by living a life of gratitude and obedience. We can do everything for his glory.

List a few of your most common, everyday activities. How can you glorify God in them?

What activities do you enjoy the most? How can you glorify God in them?

God, help me obey your Word today, not out of obligation, but rather with a heart of gratitude.

—Jonathan Byrd

Scripture Reading: Ephesians 5:15

Be very careful, then, how you live—not as unwise but as wise, making the most of every opportunity, because the days are evil.

Amanda and I tell our kids, "Look both ways before crossing the street, and be careful of traffic." We want our kids to trust us and be prepared before crossing so they don't get hurt.

In the same way, Paul warns believers to live wisely because danger is lurking. Life is difficult, evil is everywhere, and unwise living can bring unfortunate consequences.

Does this mean we need to circle the wagons and never venture out of our comfort zone? To the contrary, Paul says we are to make the most of every opportunity. Those of us furthering the kingdom of God are not playing defense—we are aggressively spreading faith, hope, and love, confident that evil has been defeated and will one day be eradicated.

What opportunities or obstacles are you facing today? How can you prepare to make the most of this day—to grow in your faith and make an eternal impact?

Life can be difficult, so we need to be in community and encourage each other. Whom can you encourage? Who consistently encourages you?

God, I love to see my kids trust and obey me. Help me to please you by walking in obedience. I confess that I don't always know how to live wisely. I pray your Holy Spirit would walk with me and be my guide.

—Jonathan Byrd

Scripture Reading: Proverbs 16:5

The LORD detests all the proud of heart.

We know how God feels about our pride. It can keep believers from becoming more like Christ, and it can cause people to reject God completely. Tim Chester says this in his book *You Can Change*:

> One of the main ways in which pride wrecks the process of change occurs when we hide our sin from others. "Whoever conceals his transgressions will not prosper, but he who confesses and forsakes them will obtain mercy" (Proverbs 28:13). We want our good reputation. So we hide, we pretend, we don't seek help…We want to avoid exposure, so we tell ourselves we can manage on our own…We love our reputation more than we hate our sin.[2]

I have experienced much growth in my own life by being truthful and vulnerable to someone else whenever I struggle. We all need to bring our sin into the light.

Be honest with yourself. Is pride or fear preventing you from revealing your weakness and growing in your faith?

What are the consequences of hiding your failures? Compare these to the consequences of vulnerability and honesty.

Lord, help me to fear you more than man and trust not in myself, but only in your Son, Jesus.

—Jonathan Byrd

2   Tim Chester, *You Can Change* (Wheaton: Crossway, 2010), 123.

Scripture Reading: Philippians 3:13-14 HCSB

Brothers, I do not consider myself to have taken hold of it. But one thing I do: forgetting what is behind and reaching forward to what is ahead, I pursue as my goal the prize promised by God's heavenly call in Christ Jesus.

Professional golfers must learn how to handle pressure-packed situations. At the end of a tournament, when all is on the line, we need to be able to trust ourselves and continue to perform effectively and efficiently.

God also wants us to finish strong for him when the pressure is on in our daily lives. Perhaps a coworker is mocking a "religion freak" in the office or a family member is challenging your Christian beliefs. Each confrontation tests us in new ways and provides new opportunities to become more like Christ.

Jesus provided the ultimate example of finishing well under extreme pressure. Invite him to walk with you in a pressure-filled situation you're facing.

What does finishing well look like in your immediate circumstance?

God, help me to know what finishing well looks like in every area of my life.

—Stewart Cink

This is an interesting explanation of why God gives us comfort during our struggles. If you were to look only at the first half of this verse, it might seem very straightforward. But the second half really throws a twist into the meaning. It doesn't say he comforts us so that we can sit back and relax. Instead, it states God's desire and command for us to comfort each other. He knows our kingdom service is most effective when we aren't overwhelmed by our troubles.

Struggle can cause us to become self-centered. But when we comfort others, we usually find that we receive comfort too!

Recall a time when you sensed God's comfort, perhaps through a friend, something you read, or a time of prayer. Do you need God's comfort today?

Does anyone you know need comforting? How can you encourage and support that person?

Dear God, thank you for comforting me in all my troubles. Show me today how to receive your comfort and how to pass it along to others.

—Stewart Cink

Scripture Reading: Hebrews 2:1 NLT

So we must listen very carefully to the truth we have heard, or we may drift away from it.

What a great verse for us in today's world, which is filled with so many distractions. The world seems to run counter to the truth on every level. We try to live for eternity, but the world bombards us with offers of instant gratification. We attempt to cultivate a spiritual worldview, but we're surrounded by materialism. We endeavor to serve others in a society that's obsessed with self.

But regardless of the distractions all around us, God is always there, never changing. He provides himself as a consistent focal point in a world that urges us to focus elsewhere. We can take a lesson from a compass. The needle always points toward north. Check your spiritual compass every day to make sure it is pointed in the right direction.

Which of the world's distractions are the most difficult for you to ignore?

What are a few ways you can check your spiritual compass?

Heavenly Father, please guide me in the right direction today. Save me from wandering away from the truth. Thank you for being my shepherd!

—Stewart Cink

Sometimes we all need a little dose of perspective. This verse reminds me of how big God's love really is, especially compared to my troubles. All he asks of us is that we love and rely on him.

When we look around us, what do we see? Is the world a threatening place, a lost cause, a source of constant irritation? Or is it filled with the knowledge of the glory of the Lord, with hints of his love everywhere and in everyone?

How much is it worth to us to live in God's love? Or how much would we risk by not? God paid quite a price for our sin—his own Son. Through his grace we receive life and a love from which we will never be separated.

Do you ever feel as if you're separated from God's love? What tends to make you feel that way?

Where can you look for hints of God's love today? Be prepared to find them in unexpected places!

Dear God, I'm likely to see whatever I expect to see. Help me to expect to see hints of your great love for me everywhere today!

—Stewart Cink

Scripture Reading: 1 Samuel 17:45-46 NLT

David replied to the Philistine, "You come to me with sword, spear, and javelin, but I come to you in the name of the LORD of Heaven's Armies—the God of the armies of Israel, whom you have defied. Today the LORD will conquer you, and I will kill you and cut off your head."

The story of David and Goliath is one of the most famous in the Bible. A young shepherd boy defeats a seasoned war veteran who was more than nine feet tall! Read the story, and you'll discover a constant theme throughout. David continually relied on God and not on himself. In the verse above, who does David say is going to conquer Goliath? The Lord! David relied on God—not only in this battle, but all throughout his life. Time and time again we see David relying on God, trusting God, seeking God. For example...

- "Whenever I am afraid I will trust in You...In God I have put my trust; I will not be afraid. What can man do to me?" (Psalm 56:3,11 NKJV).

- "The LORD is my strength and my shield; my heart trusted in Him, and I am helped" (Psalm 28:7 NKJV).

What challenges do you face today "in the name of the LORD of Heaven's Armies"?

What does "relying on God and not on yourself" mean to you in these situations?

Heavenly Father, you are the victor, and I get to follow you from victory to victory. Please guide me in the path I should go.

—Aaron Baddeley

Scripture Reading: Exodus 33:15

Then Moses said to [God], "If your Presence does not go with us, do not send us up from here."

Moses led the Israelites out of Egypt into the middle of the desert to worship God. The plan was to eventually lead them all the way to the Promised Land. Time and again the people of Israel rebelled and sinned against God, even desiring to go back to Egypt, where they had been slaves. God declared to Moses that he would give them the Promised Land, but God himself wouldn't go with them (verse 3).

Moses's response is remarkable—he desired God above all else. Moses preferred the desolate desert with God rather than the Promised Land without him. Moses knew the Promised Land had nothing to offer compared to knowing God and being in his presence.

What do you desire above all else? Does anything (family, work, hobbies, possessions…) draw your attention and focus away from God?

What does "living in God's presence" mean to you?

Lord, thank you for your promise to never leave me or forsake me. Help me to sense your presence with me today.

—Aaron Baddeley

Scripture Reading: John 19:30 NKJV

So when Jesus had received the sour wine, He said, "It is finished!" And bowing His head, He gave up His spirit.

t is finished!" These were Jesus's last words as he died on the cross, and what powerful words they were! Because of sin, man had separated himself from God. But God, in his unfailing love for us, had a plan to purchase us back. He sent his Son, Jesus, who would shed his royal blood and die on a cross to save us from slavery to sin and judgment so we could spend eternity with him. God did this for you and me because his love for us is so great that he couldn't bear the thought of living all eternity without us. This thought moves our hearts to bow down and worship him—not for what he can do for us today, but for who he is, for what he has already done, and for his unfailing love for us. Sometimes we get caught up with everything we want or think we need, but what we really need is to get back to the simplicity of the cross and always remember that "it is finished!"

When you hear Jesus saying, "It is finished," what is your reaction? Is anything keeping you from offering a worshipful response?

Jesus said, "It is finished." What does that imply about your past, present, and future shortcomings?

Jesus, thank you for finishing the work of redemption on the cross. Help me today to live as a redeemed person—full of gratitude and joy!

—Aaron Baddeley

Scripture Reading: Luke 18:27 NKJV

The things which are impossible with men are possible with God.

God excels in the realm of the seemingly impossible.

Think about all the stories in the Bible. The Red Sea parts, the sun stands still, and Jericho's walls fall down. Jesus is born of a virgin, lives a perfect life, dies, and three days later rises from the dead. Peter walks on water, lepers become clean, the blind receive sight, the lame walk…the list goes on and on. All these things are impossible for man, but with God, anything is possible. In the story of creation, all God had to do was speak, and it was done. He promised Abraham and Sarah a child when they were nearly 100 years old! Sarah laughed at the idea, and God responded by asking, "Is anything too hard for the Lord?" We need to renew our minds with this confidence—everything is possible with God!

Have you ever thought any of God's promises seemed too good to be true?

God told Paul, "My grace is sufficient for you, for My strength is made perfect in weakness" (2 Corinthians 12:9 NKJV). In what ways do you feel weak? How might God's strength be made perfect in that area?

God, help me to assess seemingly impossible situations in the light of your infinite ability.

—Aaron Baddeley

Scripture Reading: Matthew 4:18-22

As Jesus was walking beside the Sea of Galilee, he saw two brothers, Simon called Peter and his brother Andrew. They were casting a net into the lake, for they were fishermen. "Come, follow me," Jesus said, "and I will send you out to fish for people." At once they left their nets and followed him. Going on from there, he saw two other brothers, James son of Zebedee and his brother John. They were in a boat with their father Zebedee, preparing their nets. Jesus called them, and immediately they left the boat and their father and followed him.

Were these men all just waiting for something better to do? What was their first thought when Jesus called them? We'll probably never know, but we do know that they took immediate action on an adventure even though they didn't know the outcome.

We also see that they were committed. These guys weren't just sticking their toes into the water—they were all in!

Of course, we need to be careful, practice due diligence, and make wise decisions. But sometimes God calls us to follow him without knowing all the details. When he does, we need to be ready to leave some things behind to follow him on an adventure that could change our lives forever.

How might Jesus be calling you to follow him today?

Do you need to leave anything behind to follow him today?

Lord, help me take action now on a path that brings me closer to you. Show me what I need to let go of.

—Lee Janzen

Scripture Reading: John 4:34

"My food," said Jesus, "is to do the will of him who sent me and to finish his work."

Jesus had just finished a conversation with the woman at the well. She told the townspeople about Jesus, and they were so curious, they decided to go meet him themselves. As Jesus saw the crowd coming, they looked like a field that was ripe for harvest.

Meanwhile, the disciples were all about lunch.

Jesus had an unbending focus that nothing and no one could alter. He was focused on the work God had given him to do. Focused on the people he came to save. Even his physical hunger and the smell of food couldn't pull his attention away from the opportunity at hand.

Imagine what we could do with that kind of focus!

What are you focused on today? Success? Knowing God? Lunch?

Jesus's focus on God's work might have cost him lunch that day. What might following God cost you today?

Jesus, thank you for completing your mission for us. Help me clarify my mission, count the cost, and follow you wholeheartedly.

—Lee Janzen

Scripture Reading: Luke 10:40-42 NET

Martha was distracted with all the preparations she had to make, so she came up to [Jesus] and said, "Lord, don't you care that my sister has left me to do all the work alone? Tell her to help me." But the Lord answered her, "Martha, Martha, you are worried and troubled about many things, but one thing is needed. Mary has chosen the best part; it will not be taken away from her."

Martha knew Jesus was Lord, but she was too busy to enjoy his presence.

Even after we accept God's gift of grace through Christ, we still focus on earning some sort of recognition for our actions. We need to stop every now and then and remind ourselves that Jesus doesn't want us to prove our worth and value. We are already invaluable to him. He just wants us to be with him.

We are tempted to wear ourselves out working for earthly rewards, but the rewards that mean the most await us in heaven. We can have peace knowing Jesus is all the reward we need.

Have you ever caught yourself trying to impress someone? Have you ever caught yourself trying to impress God?

We all have work to do. Think of one of the activities you'll be involved in today, and picture yourself using your work as a way to worship, glorify, and partner with God.

Lord, help me focus on your presence and not on trying to impress you.

—Lee Janzen

Scripture Reading: Hebrews 8:12 NET

I will be merciful toward their evil deeds, and their sins I will remember no longer.

Imagine being able to forget every mistake you ever made on the golf course. How confidently and freely would you play? To play a shot with no fear of mistake—that would be awesome!

How much better to worship God the same way? In his presence, we are made clean. Our faith is strengthened, and our hope is renewed. Because of God's great love for us, we are no longer tied to our faults—we can live in freedom and confidence.

We can't force ourselves to forget our faults, but we can be completely cleansed from them. Are you freer and more confident than you were a year ago? If so, in what way?

When we try to hide our flaws, they continue to cause problems. But when we expose our sin and turn from it, it loses its grip on us. In what way would you like to be freer and more confident a year from now than you are today?

Lord, thank you for erasing my sin so I can come into your presence. Strengthen my faith so I can be free to be my best and bring you glory!

—Lee Janzen

Scripture Reading: 2 Corinthians 10:5

We demolish arguments and every pretension that sets itself up against the knowledge of God, and we take captive every thought to make it obedient to Christ.

This has probably been the most powerful Scripture in my life this past year. I have been making a big effort to take thoughts captive by pausing them. We need to hold thoughts in our minds and ask the Lord whether they are from him. That is the beautiful thing about communicating with the living God. He will tell you. This is a great discipline that will change our lives from the inside out.

Do you have any repeated thoughts that are not from God? Name them—confess them.

The next time you catch yourself dwelling on a negative thought, replace it with something more helpful, such as Isaiah 26:3—"You will keep in perfect peace those whose minds are steadfast, because they trust in you."

Jesus, please help me to reject thoughts that are not of you and to focus on whatever is true, whatever is noble, whatever is right, whatever is pure, whatever is lovely, whatever is admirable. My mind is a battlefield—make me aware and equip me to take my thoughts captive to your truth. Help me to experience victory in this area today!

—Ben Crane

Have you ever walked into a pitch-black room and fumbled for the light switch? As soon as you flip the switch, the darkness is dispelled, and you can see. Conversely, if you walk into a well-lit room carrying a little bit of darkness—say, in a sealed container—once you open the box, it too is flooded with light. The darkness cannot overtake the light. The light always dispels the darkness.

That's how God works. "The earth was formless and empty, and darkness was over the surface of the deep...And God said, 'Let there be light'" (Genesis 1:2-3). That's also how Jesus came into the world. He came as the light, and the darkness could not overcome it. Even today, he brings the light to any situation or problem. He shows the way. He has the answer. He lights the right path.

Where do you need Jesus's light to shine in your life today? On a confusing problem? A recurring issue? An imposing obstacle?

How can you spread the light with those around you today?

God, I open myself to you today. Shine your light into my heart and mind, my schedule and activities, and dispel any darkness in me.

—Ben Crane

Scripture Reading: Matthew 11:28 MSG

Are you tired? Worn out? Burned out on religion? Come to me. Get away with me and you'll recover your life.

Do you feel as if the more you do, the more people expect of you? Jesus's life was like that. People were all around him, literally pressing in on him and making demands of him. The more miracles he performed, the more they wanted from him. "So his fame spread...and great crowds followed him" (Matthew 4:24-25 ESV). "The whole city came out to meet Jesus" (Matthew 8:34 NKJV). "The crowds that went before him and that followed him were shouting" (Matthew 21:9 ESV). But Jesus knew he needed time away, alone with his Father, to keep focused on the primary purpose for his life here on earth. He often drew away from the crowds to be alone with God because that communion sustained him. "In the morning, having risen a long while before daylight, He went out and departed to a solitary place; and there He prayed" (Mark 1:35 NKJV).

When is the best time and where is the best place for you to stop and focus on Jesus and his Word? Try to commit to making that part of your routine.

Choose a Scripture to meditate on and even memorize today. Share it with others. Let it rejuvinate your faith walk.

I'm here, Lord. I need a few moments just to be with you. Thank you for being with me.

—Ben Crane

Scripture Reading: Hebrews 10:24-25

Let us consider how we may spur one another on toward love and good deeds, not giving up meeting together, as some are in the habit of doing, but encouraging one another—and all the more as you see the Day approaching.

Fellowship has always been an important part of the Christian journey. However, now that we can find information on any subject with a few keystrokes or mouse clicks, we can be tricked into thinking we can learn about God all on our own. This verse warns against this.

Solitary time to study God's Word is essential, but we also need time to gather with our fellow believers. Singing songs of praise is great, and so is discussing a Scripture that could be confusing to someone but very clear to another. When we hear others' perspectives, we can receive new insights about God. Likewise, we can assist others by sharing our own experiences and thoughts, which can unlock new understandings about God for them.

Assess your habits of fellowship. Are any adjustments in order?

How can you encourage others toward love and good deeds today?

Lord, thank you for my fellow believers. Help me enjoy other people's company and grow with them.

—Mark Wilson

Scripture Reading: Genesis 33:4

Esau ran to meet Jacob and embraced him; he threw his arms around his neck and kissed him. And they wept.

Twin brothers Jacob and Esau had an intense sibling rivalry. Esau was older by a few minutes, but when they were young adults, Jacob extorted the birthright from him and tricked their father, Isaac, into giving him the blessing of the firstborn. Esau was livid. Fearing for his life, Jacob fled, and the brothers were separated for about 15 years. When they were finally about to meet again, Jacob was understandably afraid and sent gifts to Esau in hopes of appeasing him.

Esau brushed the gifts aside, embraced his brother, and wept for joy, just as a long-lost brother should. I'm sure Jacob was shocked—and relieved.

Have you given up on a relationship that God might want to mend?

We all make mistakes in our relationships. Do you need to ask anyone for forgiveness? Do you need to extend forgiveness to anyone?

Lord, help me to believe you can heal relationships.

—Mark Wilson

Scripture Reading: Ephesians 4:29

Do not let any unwholesome talk come out of your mouths, but only what is helpful for building others up according to their needs, that it may benefit those who listen.

This passage begins by instructing us to avoid words that harm others. Belittling, gossiping, cursing, and yelling never build up others. What should we do instead? Hand out positive words of affirmation, like praise for a job well done or encouragement for what lies ahead.

The last part of this verse reminds us that advice is beneficial only if the recipient listens. Sometimes when people criticize me or offer advice, my first response is not to listen to them but to defend or make excuses for my behavior. With that approach, others' words aren't helpful to my future behavior at all, and I've missed an opportunity to improve.

Have you recently said something that wasn't helpful? What could you have said that would have been more beneficial?

What's the best piece of advice you've received recently?

Lord, help me carefully choose my words so that they may build up others. Also, help me receive instruction with humility, grace, and thanksgiving.

—Mark Wilson

Scripture Reading: Proverbs 28:13

Whoever conceals their sins does not prosper, but the one who confesses and renounces them finds mercy.

No one likes to be wrong. Nobody is eager to admit they made a mistake, chose poorly, or were confused. But we know we're not perfect. People make mistakes all the time.

Instead of hoping no one saw you make a mistake, why not try owning your actions, accepting responsibility, and repenting? You will be amazed at how free you feel. The consequences of holding on to your sins are far more damaging than telling the truth and asking for forgiveness. When you repent, you will feel God's grace.

Have you ever lost your patience with someone and responded with a sharp tongue? Have you ever promised something and been unable to deliver? Instead of justifying your actions, how about apologizing and asking for forgiveness? "I'm so sorry for… Will you forgive me?"

If you have children, don't forget to ask them for forgiveness. By modeling the behavior of repentance, you are letting your children know that it is all right to make mistakes and that they will always be loved and forgiven.

Do you need to confide in a trusted friend today?

How can you help your family feel free to admit their mistakes?

Lord, remind me that taking ownership of my actions will not be a sign of weakness, but of strength. Help me learn to ask for forgiveness. Thank you for your mercy and your grace.

—Mark Wilson

Scripture Reading: Ecclesiastes 11:5

As you do not know the path of the wind, or how the body is formed in a mother's womb, so you cannot understand the work of God, the Maker of all things.

God is beyond our wildest comprehension, yet he wants us to personally experience his love and express it to others. He showed us his love by sending Jesus to reconcile us to the Father.

How can we express our love to him? I believe one way is to learn about him. By getting to know God, we can better understand his desires and align our desires with his. We won't completely understand the work of God, as this verse tells us, but we can get some clarity on issues by digging a bit. Catching a glimpse of this world from God's point of view can change everything.

Be on the lookout today for clues about God's nature as you read Scripture, talk with others, serve those around you, and simply observe the world with him in mind.

God is incomprehensible. Is that a stumbling block for you? Or does it make you love him all the more? Why?

Dear Father in heaven, give me faith to trust in your ultimate plan for mankind and the universe you created.

—Mark Wilson

Scripture Reading: Jeremiah 29:12-13 ESV

You [Israel] will call upon me [God] and come and pray to me, and I will hear you. You will seek me and find me, when you seek me with all your heart.

Prayer has been confusing for me over the years. I hear of people who get up an hour early every morning to pray. Don't they get distracted by their to-do list? How do they stay awake? But I've been getting more excited about prayer recently. Here's why.

With acquaintances, I might talk about sports or the weather, but not my inner struggles or deepest desires. However, with my wife, parents, or close friends, I open up about more important issues, and therefore I enjoy a deeper relationship with them. Our bond is stronger.

The same thing happens with God. If I talk with him only about a few things, our relationship will be about as deep as a golf hole. But if I bring him all my emotions, the pleasant ones as well as the unpleasant, my bond with him will be as deep as the ocean. Prayer takes on a completely new light.

Try looking at prayer from God's point of view. He can't wait to be in a relationship with you! Keep your eyes and ears open for him to respond to you today.

What practical, realistic step can you take today toward seeking God with all your heart?

Dear God, I am going to pour out my feelings to you so we can have a more meaningful relationship. God, are you ready for this? Here goes…

—Mark Wilson

Scripture Reading: Romans 12:2

Do not conform to the pattern of this world, but be transformed by the renewing of your mind. Then you will be able to test and approve what God's will is—his good, pleasing and perfect will.

We learn from our everyday experiences and interactions, but we should be intentional about renewing our minds in other ways as well. We can either stop growing intellectually, or we can continue to expand our horizons, fill in the voids, find answers to important questions, and learn from history.

Pick a book to read that will promote your spiritual growth. If you don't know what to read, ask a trusted Christian friend or leader. Then carve out short reading times—even just five or ten minutes a day at first. You'll soon notice that you're looking at the world and conversing with God in new ways.

Consider starting a list of books you want to read. As you finish one, write just a couple of sentences of the most important things you read. Soon, your to-read list will become a journal of what you've learned!

Can you identify a Goliath in your past that you were able to defeat? Let that give you confidence that God can deliver you this time as well.

Dear Father in heaven, open my mind to learn more about you. Transform my life by the renewing of my mind.

—Mark Wilson

Scripture Reading: Romans 12:10-12,14-15 GNT

Love one another warmly as Christians, and be eager to show respect for one another. Work hard and do not be lazy. Serve the Lord with a heart full of devotion. Let your hope keep you joyful, be patient in your troubles, and pray at all times…Ask God to bless those who persecute you—yes, ask him to bless, not to curse. Be happy with those who are happy, weep with those who weep.

When I was younger, I thought of the Bible as a set of rules I needed to follow in order to be a good Christian. But during my faith journey I have realized two things.

First, I cannot earn my way to heaven, but through Christ I am saved. As a child of God, my inheritance is secure regardless of what I do. There are no rules I can follow or good works I can perform to make God love me more.

Second, if the Bible is not a set of rules, then it must be an instruction manual for living a full and happy life.

If you struggle to spend time reading the Bible, consider changing the way you read it. Do you see it as a list of rules? An invitation? The greatest rescue adventure ever? How would you describe the Bible?

Choose one of the practical exhortations in today's passage to focus on for the next 24 hours.

Dear God, thank you for the gift of the Bible. Help my eyes to see the world as you do. Help me to seek what you have prepared for me. Remind me that the Bible is a guide to living a joyful, abundant life.

—Mark Wilson

Scripture Reading: 1 Samuel 17:48

As the Philistine moved closer to attack him, David ran quickly toward the battle line to meet him.

I was feeling a little bit anxious going into a final round. Final rounds can be Goliaths at times. A couple of my believing friends drew me to the side and read to me this report that "David ran quickly toward the battle." There were three basic ways to fight in David's day—with horse and chariot, hand to hand, and with a sling. David was an expert rock slinger—he had practiced all his life. Yet the key to David's victory was not his expert rock slinging ability, but rather his confidence that God was with him in this battle.

What is your "Goliath"? What is looming on the horizon that causes you to be anxious and nervous? What can you entrust to God in this situation?

Can you identify a Goliath in your past that you were able to defeat? Let that give you confidence that God can deliver you this time as well.

God, thank you for guiding me. Fill me with confidence that as I follow you, you will lead me in victory.

—Ben Crane

Scripture Reading: John 17:23

Then the world will know that you sent me and have loved them even as you have loved me.

I just cannot get over this verse. Think about this—God loves us as much as he loves his perfect Son, Jesus!

Imagine being at a golf tournament on a Sunday. The sponsors start to give the first place trophy to the player with the best score. Suddenly they stop, find the person with the worst score, and give the trophy to him! It's radical, it doesn't make sense, it isn't right, it's backward. But this is God's love for you and for me. The Father loves you just as he loves the Son. He doesn't care what score you turn in or what you think you can do for him. He just loves you. He loves to hear what's on your heart, and he loves to see you basking in his love.

What is the appropriate response to a love like this?

With whom can you share this kind of love today? How can you do it?

God, I will be forever grateful for your radical love. I don't have the resources to love others the way you love me. Please fill me with your Spirit every day and let your love overflow in my life.

—Ben Crane

Scripture Reading: Matthew 20:28 NLT

For even the Son of Man came not to be served but to serve others and to give his life as a ransom for many.

The King of this world came to us, but he did not want to be served. He took the position of a servant—mending people's broken lives, washing his disciples' feet...even submitting to an unjust execution. He always took the humble position.

Happiness is a by-product of serving. We function best when we focus our attention on others, not ourselves.

I live a better part of my life playing tournaments. The world is different inside the ropes. If I'm not careful, I can get used to this life and even think I deserve it. The most profound thing I can do inside the ropes is to look outside the ropes for ways to serve. The by-product of this is happiness. Would I rather complain that the water in the coolers isn't cold enough, or toss a bottle over the ropes to a thirsty spectator and see a smile that makes my day?

What makes you most likely to focus on your own needs and wants instead of others'?

Whom can you serve today? How?

God, you are the eternal Creator of the universe, yet you chose to live among us as a servant. How could I, a created being, do any less? Make me more like you today.

—Ben Crane

Scripture Reading: Proverbs 15:26 GNT

The LORD hates evil thoughts, but he is pleased with friendly words.

Consider these two thoughts: (1) "Anger" is one letter away from "danger," and (2) revenge is a raging fire that consumes a person's heart.

All of us have evil thoughts about others—a discourteous driver, a person who has hurt us, or even a competitor. The thoughts do us no good, and more than that, God hates those thoughts. You can stop the downward spiral by turning evil thoughts into friendly words. Here's one way: When you're tempted to think the worst about someone, try walking in his shoes. Ask yourself, what is he feeling? What experiences might have prompted him to act that way? How can I help turn his day around?

Think of someone who sometimes makes you angry. Try walking in his shoes by asking yourself the questions above.

Arm yourself with a fresh supply of friendly words, and look for opportunities to share them today.

Lord, I know you don't want my heart churning with resentment and bitterness. Please help me turn those unpleasant thoughts into friendly words today.

—Ben Crane

Scripture Reading: Proverbs 10:17

Whoever heeds discipline shows the way to life, but whoever ignores correction leads others astray.

Who actually enjoys being corrected? Who looks forward to being disciplined? How do you respond when your spouse gives you something to consider? Do others in your life feel safe offering you suggestions?

Nearly every critique contains at least a morsel of truth. Today's Scripture tells us that the person who pays attention to constructive criticism actually moves toward life, and the one who ignores these teachable moments leads others astray.

What was the last hard truth someone spoke to you that helped you to experience more life?

How can you help others feel safe when they offer you advice?

God, help me to be so secure in your love for me that I don't feel threatened when people offer correction. Thank you for putting people in my life who love me enough to challenge me.

—Bubba Watson

Scripture Reading: Psalm 116:1-2

I love the LORD, for he heard my voice; he heard my cry for mercy. Because he turned his ear to me, I will call on him as long as I live.

Do you ever feel overwhelmed? Maybe you have more to do today than you could possibly accomplish. Perhaps something in your life seems out of control. You might be facing an obstacle that you can't imagine overcoming.

What do we do in these situations? Panic? Feel sorry for ourselves? Give up?

No. We hope, we believe, and we trust. We take our overwhelmed feelings to the Lord because he bends his ear to us! We can share the chaos of our lives with him. And somehow, just knowing that he hears us brings us peace.

Are you feeling overwhelmed or weak today? What situation are you facing?

God's ear is bent toward you right now. Briefly share your situation and your feelings with him.

O Lord, today when I'm feeling weak and incapable and overwhelmed, please give me your peace that passes understanding. Thank you for being with me!

—Bubba Watson

Scripture Reading: 1 John 4:16

We know and rely on the love God has for us. God is love. Whoever lives in love lives in God, and God in them.

Love is a decision. I know it can also be a feeling, but for today, it's a decision. Love is a decision that also leads to action. When we love something, our actions take a different course as a result.

God loves you—it's true! He knows all your inadequacies and still loves you! He proved his love by sending his Son to take your place on the cross—how's that for action! Today, live in this love. Today, may your actions be directed in all you do by this love.

Name a few things, people, and attributes of God you are loving today.

As you look back to the previous week, what actions were not in step with your living in the love of God? What changes would you like to make today?

Heavenly Father, please open my eyes today to opportunities to act out my love for you and for the people you've put in my life.

—Bubba Watson

Scripture Reading: John 1:1-5 PHILLIPS

At the beginning God expressed himself. That personal expression, that word, was with God, and was God, and he existed with God from the beginning. All creation took place through him, and none took place without him. In him appeared life and this life was the light of mankind. The light still shines in the darkness and the darkness has never put it out.

Think about the personal expression of God creating everything you will see today—every blade of grass, every grain of sand, and every person you encounter. The creativity of our Lord is awe inspiring! Yet in the midst of all the beauty you see today, there is darkness. Take courage today—the light, the personal expression of God, Jesus Christ—still shines. He shines in you today.

Where do you see God's creative genius today?

Where is one place you would like to see the light of Jesus shine today?

God, when the world seems like a frustrating place—or scary, or dark, or boring—help me to see your light in it.

—Jonathan Byrd

Scripture Reading: John 1:6-8 PHILLIPS

A man called John was sent by God as a witness to the light, so that any man who heard his testimony might believe in the light. This man was not himself the light: he was sent simply as a personal witness to that light.

It's not about you. Regardless of what your success tells you, the glory belongs to the light. You may have more talent than others, and you might have the endurance to work harder than most. But even these are gifts from God.

You are in a unique position today to be a witness to the light in every circumstance you may face. May you experience the freedom and joy of being God's witness!

How are you tempted to make this life about you and not about God?

How can you direct people's attention to God in your unique experiences today?

God, you have blessed me so much—please help me to reflect your light to others so they can give glory to you.

—Jonathan Byrd

Scripture Reading: John 1:9-10,12-13 PHILLIPS

That was the true light which shines upon every man as he comes into the world. He came into the world—the world he had created—and the world failed to recognise him...Yet wherever men did accept him he gave them the power to become sons of God. These were the men who truly believed in him, and their birth depended not on the course of nature nor on any impulse or plan of man, but on God.

You have received power to become a child of God. Your spiritual birth was not an accident or your own accomplishment. The God who created the universe chose to adopt men and women into his family, and that includes you. By believing in him, you can enjoy all the benefits of being in God's family!

Sometimes you may feel like a child of God, and sometimes you may not. Feelings are important in our experience, but at the end of the day, you belong to God either way. And that is definitely good news.

What is one benefit you have received by being a child of God?

What trait of the Father would you like implanted in your DNA today?

Father, I do believe! Thank you for empowering me to be your child. Please help me to grow into your likeness more and more each day.

—Jonathan Byrd

Scripture Reading: John 1:14,17-18 PHILLIPS

So the word of God became a human being and lived among us. We saw his splendor (the splendor as of a father's only son), full of grace and truth...For while the Law was given by Moses, love and truth came through Jesus Christ. It is true that no one has ever seen God at any time. Yet the divine and only Son, who lives in the closest intimacy with the Father, has made him known.

Everything we need to know about God and about being a man is given to us in Jesus. He is the exact representation of God (Hebrews 1:3) and the only person to have lived a perfect life (Hebrews 4:15).

Don't let beautiful paintings or stained-glass windows fool you into thinking Jesus was so otherworldly that he didn't really engage here on earth. In fact, think of the most interesting person you've ever met. Could Jesus possibly be more interesting than him or her? Yes—by far! Don't miss his incredible personality for any reason.

What is one aspect of Jesus's personality that has encouraged you?

Has anything (institutionalized religion, repeated exposure to stories about Jesus, painful experiences, personal failure) kept you from seeing the real Jesus?

Jesus, thank you for living on earth as a perfect man, for identifying with every emotion I experience, and for helping me to become more like you.

—Jonathan Byrd

Therefore, I urge you, brothers and sisters, in view of God's mercy, to offer your bodies as a living sacrifice, holy and pleasing to God—this is your true and proper worship.

What does it mean to present your body as a living and holy sacrifice?

Try using everything you experience today as an act of worship to God. Your interactions with a barista, a client, a golfing buddy; your relationships with your family, your coworkers, your boss; your activities on the job, around the house, at the gym… do everything with God, giving thanks to him. Everything you do can be an act of worship if you do it in relationship with him!

Is anything about this Scripture challenging to you? If so, what? Why?

Often we think of worship as singing in church, but here Paul suggests that offering our bodies as a sacrifice to God is in fact worshipping. What is one thing you will do with your physical body today as an act of worship to God?

Lord, I offer my body as a sacrifice today. May I be holy and pleasing to you in everything I do, and may I honor and worship you in every activity today.

—Zach Johnson

Listen to this verse from the perspective of commentator C.E.B. Cranfield: "And stop letting yourselves be conformed to this age, but continue to let yourselves be transformed by the renewing of your mind."

We might assume that the transformation Paul talks about is something we do. It isn't. Instead, it is something God does in us. Our spiritual disciplines cannot bring about transformation. We cannot pray enough, study enough, or memorize enough to transform ourselves. We can cooperate with God, only he can transform us by renewing our minds.

What is the pattern of this world? How do you let yourself be conformed to it?

How has God renewed your mind—what methods has he used—so that you can be transformed and able to know his will?

Lord, I pray that you will transform my mind so that I may be able to see clearly your will. May I not conform to what this world wants of me. Rather, may I be conformed to your image.

—Zach Johnson

Scripture Reading: Romans 12:3

For by the grace given me I say to every one of you: Do not think of yourself more highly than you ought, but rather think of yourself with sober judgment, in accordance with the faith God has distributed to each of you.

This is a tough one. We are naturally separated from God, so we are selfish and think about our own good and welfare before thinking about others and God. As a PGA tour pro, I can easily fall into the trap of thinking too highly of myself. We all have special skills or achievements, but God isn't as impressed by these things as most folks are. He is much more concerned with our faith in him and how we live it out—especially in the way we treat other people. As God gives us more faith, he will give us broader platforms to share it.

How do you measure success in your own life?

How is God building your faith in him?

Lord, I pray that I would not think too highly of myself. Instead, Lord, I pray that you would increase my faith.

—Zach Johnson

Scripture Reading: Romans 12:4-8

Just as each of us has one body with many members, and these members do not all have the same function, so in Christ we, though many, form one body, and each member belongs to all the others. We have different gifts, according to the grace given to each of us. If your gift is prophesying, then prophesy in accordance with your faith; if it is serving, then serve; if it is teaching, then teach; if it is to encourage, then give encouragement; if it is giving, then give generously; if it is to lead, do it diligently; if it is to show mercy, do it cheerfully.

Paul is describing the church, the body of Christ. He uses the analogy of a healthy human body with its different parts all working together.

God has given you unique gifts and abilities to function as a part of his body for his purpose. Only when we are doing what God has called us to do will we find the satisfaction, fulfillment, and joy we seek. As we serve him, he gives us strength, and we are able to do immeasurably more than we imagine. God is not asking us to do this alone, only to do what he has empowered us to do.

As you look at the list in this passage, what jumps out at you? What are a couple of the gifts God has given you?

How can you use your gifts to build up others and glorify God today?

Lord, give me insight into my gifts and how you would have me use those gifts to serve others today.

—Zach Johnson

Scripture Reading: Matthew 5:3

Blessed are the poor in spirit, for theirs is the kingdom of heaven.

Blessed are the broken. Blessed are the empty. Blessed are those who are bankrupt...

I am most blessed when I realize that I have nothing without Jesus. Our self-sufficiency is one of the main things that keep us from him. In so many areas of our lives, we think we don't really need Jesus. This is the great lie of Satan. Welcome your brokenness for what it is—a direct path to Jesus. And think about this promise—those who recognize their emptiness and turn to Jesus will breathe the air of heaven 24/7.

Reflect on a time in your life when God was faithful in your emptiness.

Has God used your brokenness to bless others? If so, how?

Thank you for loving all of me, Jesus, and using my story to bless others. Protect me from pride and let my brokenness be a signpost to you.

—Ben Crane

Whoever wants to become great among you must be your servant, and whoever wants to be first must be your slave—just as the Son of Man did not come to be served, but to serve, and to give his life as a ransom for many.

We like to be served, especially as we travel. We are served on the plane, served at the hotel, and served at restaurants. Look back on yesterday for a moment—think of all the ways people served you.

What does kingdom leadership look like? Look for ways to serve. We become great by serving the people God puts in our path. We serve our family, we serve our coworkers and supervisors, we serve our friends and fellow church members. This is a hard concept to grasp because our culture bombards us with messages that we deserve to be served. But Jesus served us to the point of dying for us. As we become more like him, we serve others, even if reducing their suffering causes us to suffer a little more.

Given your unique skills, opportunities, and relationships, what is a good way for you to serve someone today?

What obstacles will you likely have to overcome in order to serve others today?

Lord, open my eyes today to all the opportunities you have given me to serve. Help me die to myself and serve you.

—Cameron Tringale

Scripture Reading: Luke 12:48

From everyone who has been given much, much will be demanded; and from the one who has been entrusted with much, much more will be asked.

Sometimes I wonder if God smiles as he entrusts us with possessions, relationships, abilities, and opportunities.

A pastor who was traveling had an opportunity to briefly talk with his taxi driver about God. When the pastor reached his destination, the taxi driver gave him too much change. The pastor caught the mistake and returned the extra money. The cab driver said, "I did that on purpose. I wanted to see if what you said about God was for real or an act."

Who knows what opportunities we will have today to be faithful with that which God has entrusted to us!

What has God given you? Take a moment to make a mental list and thank God for what he has given you.

Today, how can you demonstrate faithfulness with something God has given you?

Lord, help me to use all that you have given to me for your glory today, tomorrow, and forever!

—Cameron Tringale

Scripture Reading: Galatians 6:9

Let us not become weary in doing good, for at the proper time we will reap a harvest if we do not give up.

Do nice guys finish last? We write the check and never get a thank you. We let the car into the traffic and get no wave. We loan our car or home and get it back worse than when we loaned it. The list could go on and on.

But every time you do good, you plant a seed. We don't know how or when, but "at the proper time" these little acts of "doing good" will come back to us in the form of blessings. Doing good bears fruit! Today's Scripture encourages us to not get tired of doing good. Hang in there, and take the long view—good will eventually come back to you!

Have you had opportunities for "doing good" in the past few weeks? Are you motivated to continue, or are you growing slightly weary?

God sees every act of kindness and will reward you in this life or in the next. Today, as you do good for someone, remember that God is with you and will reward you.

Lord, help me and those around me today to not grow weary of doing good!

—Cameron Tringale

Scripture Reading: Acts 20:28 NASB

Be on guard for yourselves and for all the flock, among which the Holy Spirit has made you overseers, to shepherd the church of God which He purchased with His own blood.

I see two thoughts in this verse. (1) Be on guard. The evil one wants to take you out. Note where you are most susceptible to attack and do whatever is necessary to stand firm in your faith. (2) Others are counting on you. People are looking to you for leadership—your family, coworkers, friends, fellow worshippers...Your faithfulness to God is a tremendous blessing to other people.

How important is this? God paid a huge price for our salvation—"his own blood." God made our victory over evil his number one priority. How could we do any less?

Whom has God placed in your flock? How are they doing? Is he is asking you to do anything for your flock?

How can you "be on guard" today? What are a few of your most vulnerable areas, and how can you strengthen them?

Lord, help me to be on guard—for my sake as well as the good of those who are watching me.

—Cameron Tringale

Scripture Reading: Luke 10:41-42

"Martha, Martha," the Lord answered, "you are worried and upset about many things, but few things are needed—or indeed only one. Mary has chosen what is better, and it will not be taken away from her."

Our Lord's greatest desire is for us to be with him.

We all have many responsibilities to fulfill and challenges to overcome. Our schedules and to-do lists are overflowing with important events and tasks. Jesus lifts up Mary's example not so that we might ignore our various assignments, but so that we will prioritize our most valuable opportunity—to sit at his feet and hear what he has to say.

Peace, love, and joy are ours only when we prioritize being with Jesus.

Describe a time when you enjoyed being alone with Jesus.

What obstacles must you overcome to do the one thing that matters?

Lord Jesus, in every season of my life, help me to prioritize time with you above every competing thought, ambition, worry, or distraction.

—Ben Crane

Scripture Reading: Acts 4:13

When they saw the courage of Peter and John and realized that they were unschooled, ordinary men, they were astonished and they took note that these men had been with Jesus.

The most important word in all the English language might be "with."

Read this Scripture one more time. Peter, who earlier denied his Lord, is now described as courageous. John, who was passed over for rabbi school, is now rivaling the religious academics. What happened?

They had been with Jesus. They lived with him for three years and spoke with him after his resurrection from the dead.

How has being with Jesus changed you?

What might help you remember throughout the day that Jesus is with you?

Jesus, thank you for being with me every moment of every day. Help me set aside special times to focus on being with you.

—Ben Crane

Scripture Reading: 2 Timothy 2:11

Here is a trustworthy saying: If we died with him, we will also live with him.

I will never forget the day I realized Jesus died on the cross for me. Unfortunately, I have said or heard the words "Jesus died for you" so many times that they don't have the same effect on me now that they did when I was five years old. It was a huge deal—he died for me!

Still, when I allow myself to go there, I realize my place is right next to him on the cross. My life has meaning today because of my identification with Jesus. My old life, which was separated from God, died with Christ. My new life, which is forever hid with Christ in God, rose with him on Easter morning. I can look forward to being with God in this life and the next!

List a few ways that your own new life in Christ is different from your old life.

What does living with him today mean to you?

Jesus, I can never thank you enough for experiencing death so we can experience life! Help me to remember throughout this day that I am living with you.

—Ben Crane

Scripture Reading: Mark 12:30

Love the Lord your God with all your heart and with all your soul and with all your mind and with all your strength.

A friend of mine says that Jesus wants us to give him that which matters most to us—our hearts. I think he wants even more than that!

The great news is that our Lord is patient. He waits until you are ready to give him the next piece of your life. Perhaps all you can give him is this day. Maybe he is asking you to entrust your family to him in a new way. He might be asking you to place your future more completely in his hands.

Loving God with all your heart, soul, mind, and strength is a process. Don't worry if you're not all the way there yet. Take whatever step of faith you can, and trust that God, who is patient, is delighted in that—and in you!

What does loving God with all your heart mean to you? All your soul? All your mind? All your strength?

Do you sense anything holding you back in any of these areas? Talk with your patient, loving Lord about that.

God, I want to love you with all that I am, but I can tell that my love for you is often imperfect. Thank you for being patient, for working with me, for loving me!

—Ben Crane

Scripture Reading: Romans 1:17

For in the gospel the righteousness of God is revealed—a righteousness that is by faith from first to last, just as it is written: "The righteous will live by faith."

Faith from first to last! Faith in the living Jesus Christ brought us out of death into life, and that same faith carries us through life. The works we do don't give us life—they are a result of our new life in Christ. We experience this life simply by believing in the resurrected, living Christ, who saved us apart from anything we did or will ever do!

Is fully trusting God with your life more difficult in some areas than in others? In what area of your life would you like to trust God more today?

If you're not certain what you believe, relax. You are in the right place at the right time for spiritual growth. What is one thing you can do today to take a step of faith with God?

Lord, I do believe—help me overcome my unbelief. Thank you for helping me to live by faith in you.

—Zach Johnson

These two verses are fascinating. In 24 words John lays out the gospel. Why is Jesus called the Word? Just as our words explain our thoughts to others, so the Son of God came to reveal his Father's mind to the world.

The Word, Jesus, existed as God *before* time and space. He was there in the beginning with God when everything was made. And the Word, Jesus, existed as a man *in* time and space. He came and lived with us when we were estranged from God. He alone was qualified to accomplish our salvation.

Take a minute to reflect on the fact that Jesus "knitted you together in your mother's womb" for a specific purpose. How does that make you feel?

Jesus is God's way of speaking to his people. Take a minute and pray to Jesus that you would hear his voice. Be open to the creative ways he gets your attention.

Jesus, thank you for knowing me and becoming like me so I could know you and become more like you.

—Zach Johnson

The word "fear" has several meanings.

To fear the Lord is to revere him, to be in awe of him, to understand that he is God and we are not. Thus this fear is actually compatible with the highest form of love for God. That love is the start of knowledge and wisdom! Fools are people who have no solid foundation of wisdom. They're as fickle as the wind because they have no regard for God.

What is the difference between fearing disaster and fearing the Lord?

Think of someone you respect because of their godly wisdom. How would you describe that person?

Lord, you are more wonderful than I could ever imagine. I am in awe of you, I joyfully submit myself to you, and I pray you'll help me grow in my healthy fear of the Lord.

—Zach Johnson

Scripture Reading: Ephesians 3:17-19

May [Christ] dwell in your hearts through faith. And I pray that you, being rooted and established in love, may have power, together with all the Lord's holy people, to grasp how wide and long and high and deep is the love of Christ, and to know this love that surpasses knowledge—that you may be filled to the measure of all the fullness of God.

Notice the apostle Paul's emphasis on God's love. He prayed that the believers in Ephesus would be rooted and established in God's love, have power to grasp the dimensions of God's love, and know God's love—even though it surpasses knowledge. Paul was convinced that if these Christians were completely immersed in God's love, they would be filled with the fullness of God!

God may have many characteristics, but he *is* love. If we want God to fill us, we do well to think long and deep about his great love for us!

Do you ever feel as if God is mad at you, tired of you, disappointed in you? Ask him to dispel those lies with the truth—he loves you more than you can imagine!

How might you become more completely rooted and established in God's love?

Father, thank you for loving me! I confess that sometimes I wonder what you think of me. Help me to chase away those doubts with the truth!

—Zach Johnson

Scripture Reading: Philippians 4:6-7

Do not be anxious about anything, but in every situation, by prayer and petition, with thanksgiving, present your requests to God. And the peace of God, which transcends all understanding, will guard your hearts and your minds in Christ Jesus.

To be anxious is to worry or be nervous. When we face a challenge and don't know how it will turn out, we tend to fear the worst. But when we are confident that we are secure in our loving God's hands, we are assured that he knows what is happening and will use all things for our good. So Paul suggests that by continually presenting our requests to God in prayer and thanks, we will experience his peace, which transcends understanding. This peace guards our hearts (our frayed emotions) and minds (our fearful thoughts) by wrapping everything around Christ Jesus.

This is the best antidote for toxic worry and nervousness.

Are you anxious about anything right now? Name it and by prayer and petition present your request to God.

Have you ever walked through a potentially stressful situation while experiencing supernatural peace? If not, ask God for his peace the next time you face a challenge.

God, whenever I experience anxiety, help me remember to present my requests to you and to give you thanks.

—Ben Crane

Scripture Reading: John 7:17-18

Anyone who chooses to do the will of God will find out whether my teaching comes from God or whether I speak on my own. Whoever speaks on their own does so to gain personal glory, but he who seeks the glory of the one who sent him is a man of truth; there is nothing false about him.

Jesus highlights two life-changing choices we make every day.

First, do we live to do God's will? Before we have all the facts, before we assess all the options, before we know all the consequences...do we decide beforehand that we will do God's will no matter what? When we make that decision, the truth (the facts and information) will fall into place.

Second, do we seek God's glory? People who put themselves first often end up distorting the truth to make themselves look good. But when we seek God's glory, we are committed to the truth.

Living for God's will and living for God's glory—these are two of the best choices we can make.

What decisions do you need to make in the near future? How might God's will and God's glory play into those decisions?

Have considerations of God's will and God's glory led you to make any difficult decisions in the past? What happened?

God, strengthen me to do your will every day. Let your glory shine through me so that others will be drawn to you.

—Cameron Tringale

When the apostle Paul says we are God's "handiwork," he uses the Greek word *poiema*. We are God's poem, his masterpiece, crafted and shaped by him as an expression of his incredible grace.

But God didn't create us to hang us on a wall in a museum. We are living poems, walking and breathing masterpieces, designed to perform the beautiful acts that he has prepared in advance for us to do. Acts of goodness and kindness and mercy. Acts of faith and hope and love. Acts that reflect the nature of our Creator.

As God's handiwork, we have inestimable value and unparalleled purpose and meaning.

What's the difference between being conceited and seeing yourself as God's masterpiece?

Do any of your daily tasks seem meaningless? Imagine yourself performing your duties as good works that he has given you to do so you can reflect his character.

God, I confess that I rarely feel like much of a masterpiece. Help me to look past the surface and to see how you are renewing your image in me.

—Ben Crane

Scripture Reading: John 1:14 PHILLIPS

The word of God became a human being and lived among us. We saw his splendour (the splendour as of a father's only son), full of grace and truth.

Jesus was and is full of grace and truth.

Grace has never been more perfectly demonstrated than in the life, death, and resurrection of Christ. When we were completely unable to restore our broken relationship with God, he became a man and reconciled humanity to himself. Now we can live in the freedom of God's grace every day.

And Jesus is the truth. Truth is a person. When we walk with Jesus, we walk in the truth. He demonstrated the amazing truth about God when he lived among us. His transforming work in our lives reveals the truth that he is alive and active in our lives today.

Think about God's gift of grace. Have you allowed yourself to receive grace from Jesus or others lately? Do you need to show grace or give grace to others or even to yourself?

How can your life be a demonstration of the truth today?

Lord, may I live fully in your grace and truth today, trusting in the freedom I experience in you through both!

—Cameron Tringale

Scripture Reading: John 1:49-50 PHILLIPS

Nathanael exclaimed, "Master, you are the Son of God, you are the king of Israel!" "Do you believe in me," replied Jesus, "because I said I had seen you underneath that fig tree? You are going to see something greater than that!"

It's easy to chalk up situations in our lives to coincidence or chance. Nathaniel could easily have scoffed at Jesus's words. God is revealing himself to us on a daily basis, but we often miss the signs of his presence. Sometimes we aren't looking for them, and sometimes we aren't willing to admit they're from him.

If you were trying to find your keys or a remote control, would you sit on the couch and say, "Boy, I hope they turn up"? No, you would search up and down, checking every place you could think of. Jesus isn't hiding or misplaced, but the principle is the same—we can look for Christ's presence everywhere. And when we see him, we can give him thanks.

Stop, take a breath, reflect back on the past few days, and ask yourself, "Lord, where are you working in and around me?"

Remember the moments in your past when you've seen God clearly at work. Celebrate one or two of those with a friend or a loved one.

Lord, thank you for the ways you reveal yourself. Please give me eyes to see your hand and ears to hear your voice in my life.

—Ben Crane

Scripture Reading: John 15:13 PHILLIPS

There is no greater love than this—that a man should lay down his life for his friends.

We were not meant to live life alone. Having people around us and being in community—these are essential. These people speak into our lives, knowing our thoughts and feelings, our hopes and dreams. Likewise, we do the same for them! Friendship at its best is selfless—it is a ministry. Friends grieve each other's losses, comfort each other in times of sorrow, and celebrate each other's victories. Sometimes all it takes is simply being available and present. Moreover, by loving and caring for one another, we actually proclaim Christ to others (John 13:34-35).

Friendship among believers distinguishes us from the rest of the world. True love and true friendship require us to lay down our lives and sacrifice—something we rarely see in today's world.

Do you have a friend or two you can grieve with, share comfort with, and celebrate with?

How might you be able to lay down your life for someone today?

God, your love has completely transformed my life. Help me to love others today the way you have sacrificially loved me.

—Ben Crane

Scripture Reading: 1 John 3:18

Dear children, let us not love with words or speech but with actions and in truth.

Actions speak louder than words.

Words of love are important. Our words are to be full of grace and mercy. We build each other up and strengthen our relationships by speaking words of love. But if our words aren't backed up with actions, they can ring hollow or sound fake.

People can doubt our words, but it's tough to argue with an act of kindness. Sometimes our words get all tangled up, but our actions speak loud and clear. And sometimes we say things just because we think we're supposed to. But when we get involved and take action, we participate in God's love for another person, and we become more like Jesus in the process.

Does someone need an act of kindness today? What simple thing can you do?

What does loving someone "in truth" mean to you?

Heavenly Father, open my eyes today to opportunities to love people with my actions.

—Davis Love III

This is the prayer of a man who is desperate to know God. He pleads with God to teach him his ways so he can walk in the truth of who God is. Another translation says, "Give me an undivided heart." The psalmist knows he's prone to wander from God and needs God to continually transform his heart.

He asks for divine help with confidence because he has a special relationship with God. Did you notice how he calls him "my God"? There is no distance here. He's speaking not only to the cosmic Creator but also to his personal Lord.

Philippians 1:6 says, "He who began a good work in you will bring it to completion at the day of Jesus Christ" (ESV). What work is God doing in you right now?

Have you ever felt as if your heart is divided? (Who hasn't!) How can a busy person have an undivided heart?

O Lord my God, thank you for helping me shape my heart. My desire is to know you. Teach me your way so I may joyfully walk with you and bring you glory.

—Cameron Tringale

Scripture Reading: Matthew 14:27-30 ESV

Jesus spoke to them, saying, "Take heart; it is I. Do not be afraid."
And Peter answered him, "Lord, if it is you, command me to come
to you on the water." He said, "Come." So Peter got out of the
boat and walked on the water and came to Jesus. But when he
saw the wind, he was afraid, and beginning to sink he cried out,
"Lord, save me."

When we have a relationship with Jesus and are following him, we aren't judged by the amount of faith we have, but instead, by whom our faith is in.

We aren't likely to see anyone walk on water, but we probably have witnessed people do amazing things when they were focused on Christ. But when Peter looked away from Jesus and started wondering about what might happen, he began to sink. The good news is, Peter was able to cry out to Jesus.

Whether we're floating along or starting to sink, we can do the same.

Has Jesus ever asked you to step out of your boat and into a potentially scary situation? What happened?

As you look ahead to the rest of your day, what situations do you foresee that might pull your attention away from Jesus?

Lord Jesus, I believe anything is possible with you. Help me fix my mind on you alone. Work through me today in a way that brings you all the glory.

—Cameron Tringale

Scripture Reading: Titus 3:3-5 ESV

For we ourselves were once foolish, disobedient, led astray, slaves to various passions and pleasures, passing our days in malice and envy, hated by others and hating one another. But when the goodness and loving kindness of God our Savior appeared, he saved us.

Foolish, disobedient, enslaved to passions, malicious, envious... Does this describe someone you'd want to spend time with? Probably not. Does it sound familiar—does it sound like you? Hopefully it doesn't, but the truth is, this is the story of every one of us. We all lived this way before the Lord revealed himself to us and gave us eyes to see and know him. Paul is writing to Christians and reminding them how they lived before God saved them.

Let's not miss the last few words of these verses. God is the one who does the saving. We were stuck pursuing our passions and pleasures, but our good God called us out of that slavery and into relationship with him.

Take a moment and consider your life before you met Jesus. Which of Paul's words can you relate to? In what area have you experienced the most growth?

Goodness and loving-kindness are attributes of God. What do those things mean to you?

Lord, I thank you for your loving-kindness. You indeed are good to rescue us from ourselves and reconcile us to yourself through your Son. Be with us today and help us remember our new life, which we live with you and for you.

—Cameron Tringale

Scripture Reading: 1 Peter 1:3-5 ESV

Blessed be the God and Father of our Lord Jesus Christ! According to his great mercy, he has caused us to be born again to a living hope through the resurrection of Jesus Christ from the dead, to an inheritance that is imperishable, undefiled, and unfading, kept in heaven for you, who by God's power are being guarded through faith for a salvation ready to be revealed in the last time.

Our world is obsessed with fancy cars, big houses, designer jewelry, new clothes, and other things that end up in garage sales. We rightfully enjoy these blessings from God, but they will eventually lose their shine. They don't have lasting value.

But through the resurrection of Christ, we have new life and a living hope—things that last forever! We can find joy in these things regardless of our current circumstances. Whether we are being praised or persecuted, in times of testing or resting, we can always celebrate our new life in Christ and the wonderful inheritance awaiting us.

What has God blessed you with recently? Thank God for his provision.

What difficulty are you facing? If you can, practice rejoicing in your living hope even in the midst of this situation.

Father, thank you for giving me new life through Jesus's finished work on the cross. You've given me an inheritance that will not fade or rust—eternity with your Son!

—Cameron Tringale

Scripture Reading: Acts 24:16

I strive always to keep my conscience clear before God and man.

God gave you and me a gift—a conscience. Amazingly, people from every walk of life tend to know what is right, what is wrong, and what is a bit gray. Where does this knowledge come from?

The apostle Paul testified that he worked hard to keep his conscience clear. How? It's not complicated. Do the right thing, follow the Holy Spirit's leading, and when something appears to be gray, steer clear! A clear conscience is more valuable than whatever may be tempting you. And at the resurrection of those who have trusted in Christ, you will be rewarded for every decision you made to live a righteous life.

Is anything keeping you from having a clear conscience? If so, read 1 John 1:9 and experience God's wonderful cleansing!

Are you "striving" to keep your conscience clear before God? How?

God, thank you for the tremendous gift of my conscience. Help me to treasure this gift—to keep my conscience clear and to do what I know is right.

—Davis Love III

Scripture Reading: Matthew 5:16

Let your light shine before others, that they may see your good deeds and praise your Father in heaven.

Have you ever tried to hide a light? It's hard to do—light always penetrates the darkness.

God is asking us to let our light shine by living our lives right out in front of the world, hiding nothing. Doing good things and saying good things will keep you free of regrets and will bring praise to God. When you let your light shine before others by doing good deeds right out in the open, you aren't drawing undue attention to yourself. Rather, you're acting like a mirror, reflecting God's glory to people and people's praise to God!

Today let a couple good deeds penetrate the darkness. Don't hide your light under a bushel—let it shine!

What good deed have you thought about doing? What keeps you from doing it today?

Have you ever praised God for a good deed someone performed for you?

God, help me get over my reticence to do good deeds in plain sight. Help me focus on you and not myself so I can shine brightly for you.

—Davis Love III

Scripture Reading: Genesis 1:1,3

In the beginning God created the heavens and the earth...And God said, "Let there be light," and there was light.

God spoke, and it was done. To create this whole universe, this wonderful world we live in, all he had to do was say the word, and it was done—perfectly. Reflect on that for a minute. Think about the power and authority of God's words.

When we read our Bibles, we are reading God's written Word, which has the same power and authority that his word had at creation. God is the same yesterday, today, and forever— which means that his word also does not change. When Satan tempted Jesus in the desert, how did Jesus reply? Jesus said every time, "It is written." He quoted Scripture, and every time Satan had no answer. Why? Because of the power and authority of God's Word. The Word of God has many promises in it—promises of peace, love, forgiveness, healing, strength, acceptance, and most of all, eternal life. If we are fully convinced the Bible is God's Word, we can quote it as Jesus did and see it change our lives.

What temptation are you facing today? What passage of Scripture can you draw from to receive strength to win this battle? If you can't think of one, ask your pastor or Bible study leader.

What passage of Scripture has recently spoken to you?

God, thank you for the gift of the Scriptures, and thank you for speaking to me through them today.

—Aaron Baddeley

Scripture Reading: James 1:6-8 ESV

But let him ask in faith, with no doubting, for the one who doubts is like a wave of the sea driven and tossed by the wind. For that person must not suppose that he will receive anything from the Lord; he is a double-minded man, unstable in all his ways.

How do we receive wisdom from the Lord? Through faith, with no doubting.

Through our faith in God, we received salvation and the forgiveness of our sins. We trusted in him alone and not in anything we could do to save ourselves. Similarly, when we need wisdom from God, we depend on him completely, confident that he will fulfill his promise.

Doubt makes us double-minded and unstable. God still wants to give us wisdom, but our connection with him—our faith—breaks up as we vacillate from one mindset to another.

Conversely, faith makes us single-minded and stable. When God's Word is the foundation of our lives, it guides us, encourages us, and empowers us to stand strong.

How do we build our faith and become single-minded? Read Romans 10:17.

What decision are you facing? Ask God for wisdom and for him to speak to you through the Scriptures.

God, I commit to keep my connection with you—my faith—clear and strong today. Thank you for your promise to give me wisdom when I need it.

—Aaron Baddeley

Scripture Reading: Hosea 6:4,6 NKJV

O Ephraim, what shall I do to you? O Judah, what shall I do to you? For your faithfulness is like a morning cloud, and like the early dew it goes away...For I desire mercy and not sacrifice, and the knowledge of God more than burnt offerings.

Why was God concerned with Ephraim (Israel—the northern kingdom) and Judah (the southern kingdom)?

Their faithfulness disappeared like morning clouds and dew. These two things vanish with the sun's heat. Scripture often uses fire and heat to describe times of testing or trials. The apostle Peter refers to our faith being tested by fire (1 Peter 1:6-7). When the temperature rises in our lives, our faithfulness to God shouldn't melt away. If anything, we should become more resolute.

Faithfulness is steadiness in our allegiance to God and our affection for him. God's desire is not for us to waver, but to be steady, to be consistent—to walk with him daily, spending time with him, reading his Word, talking to him in prayer, looking to him, and relying on him. God delights in our faithfulness to him!

How can you demonstrate your faithfulness to God today?

What challenges your faithfulness? How can you overcome those challenges?

God, I know faith is a gift, but I see that it's also a commitment. Strengthen my resolve to be a faithful follower of Christ.

—Aaron Baddeley

Scripture Reading: Proverbs 3:3 NKJV

Let not mercy and truth forsake you; bind them around your neck, write them on the tablet of your heart.

Our hearts are like tablets. What's written on them?

Here Solomon says to make sure that mercy and truth are written on the tablet of our hearts. So far so good—but what else is written on our hearts? Resentment? Unforgiveness? Doubt? Pride? Or what about love? Faith? Joy? Peace?

Solomon also instructs us, "Above all else, guard your heart, for everything you do flows from it" (Proverbs 4:23). "Above all else"—nothing is more important. The things we write on our hearts shape our lives—how we think, what we feel, and how we act. If unforgiveness is written on our hearts, we'll struggle to forgive people and see the best in them. But if love is written on our hearts, we'll see the best in them, care for them, and be quick to forgive them and move on.

Can Jesus erase some things from our hearts and help us write something new? Yes he can! He can change bitterness to thankfulness, unforgiveness to love. Our job is to guard our hearts.

How do things get written on the tablet of your heart?

If your heart were a tablet, what things would be written near the top or in the biggest, boldest letters?

God, show me what's written on the tablet of my heart. I choose to guard my heart from anything that leads me away from you.

—Aaron Baddeley

Scripture Reading: 1 John 5:4 NKJV

Whatever is born of God overcomes the world. And this is the victory that has overcome the world—our faith.

love the word "whatever" in this verse. Anything born of God—a plan, a word, his Word, family, golf, business, life—whatever is born of God overcomes the world.

How can we be so confident? We know that "He who is in you is greater than he who is in the world" (1 John 4:4 NKJV). Because of Jesus's victory on the cross, the battle is already won.

As followers of Jesus, we want only "whatever is born of God." Whatever is not born of God will suffer defeat and have no eternal value. As we cooperate with God, we experience victory, and our actions are filled with meaning.

But this doesn't mean overcoming will always be easy. The world will do anything to discourage us. But the good news is, our faith overcomes the world! We win when we believe in Christ's work on the cross and the promises of God's Word.

What in your life is born of God? What isn't?

What challenges are you currently facing? We win when we believe—what does winning mean in your current situation?

Heavenly Father, show me anything in my life that isn't born of you. Thank you for securing our ultimate victory over the world. Help me to overcome by believing in you.

—Aaron Baddeley

Scripture Reading: John 4:34 NKJV

Jesus said to them, "My food is to do the will of Him who sent Me, and to finish His work."

Jesus was nourished and fulfilled by doing the work of his heavenly Father and bringing it to completion. Just before Jesus died on the cross, he said, "It is finished." Jesus knew God's plan, and he knew that he had completed all that the Father wanted him to do. Jesus often said that he could do only what he saw his Father doing.

God has a plan for your life too. King David prayed, "You saw me before I was born. Every day of my life was recorded in your book. Every moment was laid out before a single day had passed" (Psalm 139:16 NLT). God told the people of Jerusalem, "I know the plans I have for you" (Jeremiah 29:11). Jesus appeared to Paul on the road to Damascus and told him about God's plan for his life (Acts 26:14-18). God's plan for your life is just as important as his plan for anyone else's life. His plan will empower you to be a light for him and to tell people about Jesus.

Frederick Buechner wrote, "The place God calls you to is the place where your deep gladness and the world's deep hunger meet." Where do those intersect in your life?

At the end of this day, will you be able to say, "I have finished the work God gave me to do today"?

Heavenly Father, help me to know the work you have for me to do, and empower me to do my part today.

—Aaron Baddeley

Scripture Reading: 2 Timothy 4:17 NKJV

The Lord stood with me and strengthened me, so that the message might be preached fully through me.

Three things stand out in this passage. First, the Lord stood with Paul. I picture Jesus and Paul standing together strong and tall with their arms linked, ready for whatever is coming their way.

Second, the Lord strengthened him. The Lord didn't do Paul's work, but the Lord strengthened Paul to do the work. This is such an encouraging Scripture. Paul wrote half the books in the New Testament, performed many miracles for Jesus, and preached all over the known world, yet he still needed help. He needed Jesus to come alongside him, to stand with him, to strengthen him so that he could do what Jesus wanted him to do.

And third, why did Jesus stand with Paul and strengthen him? "So that the message might be preached fully through me," Paul said.

Jesus will stand with you and strengthen you to accomplish the tasks he's given you to do. Jesus won't do the work for you, but he'll empower you to do more than you could ever do on your own.

Make a mental list of the places you will be today. Picture Jesus walking alongside you.

What do you need God's strength to do today?

Lord, thank you for standing with me, strengthening me, and empowering me to do more than I could possibly do on my own.

—Aaron Baddeley

Scripture Reading: Colossians 2:6-7 NKJV

As you therefore have received Christ Jesus the Lord, so walk in Him, rooted and built up in Him and established in the faith, as you have been taught, abounding in it with thanksgiving.

Scripture compares believers to trees (Psalm 1:3; Jeremiah 17:8). If a tree has shallow roots, it won't be able to withstand a windstorm, but will be uprooted. In times of drought, it will wither and die. On the other hand, if that tree has deep roots, it will withstand strong winds. In arid times, it will find refreshment in the moist soil deep beneath the surface.

Similarly, if we want to withstand storms and dry times, we need to make sure we are deeply rooted in God. To continue bearing fruit, we must develop our root system by spending time alone with God in prayer and the Scriptures.

No one who sees a tree says, "Those are some good-looking roots!" No, they see the leaves, the branches, the fruit. In the same way, people won't see you deepening your relationship with Christ through time alone with him, but they'll see the results. They'll see you standing strong through stormy times. They'll see your love, your joy, your peace. They'll see your good works and glorify God because they'll know you are rooted in Christ.

How will you deepen your roots in Jesus today?

What storms have you faced or might you be facing soon?

God, thank you for nourishing me every day. Help me to be rooted and built up in you and established in the faith.

—Aaron Baddeley

Scripture Reading: Psalm 63:1 NKJV

O God, You are my God; early will I seek You; my soul thirsts for You, my flesh longs for You in a dry and thirsty land where there is no water.

This is one of my all-time favorite verses. Hear the cry of David's heart. Every bone in his body longs for God and desires him—not for what God can do for him, but for who God is. In verse 5, David says, "My soul shall be satisfied," even in a dry and thirsty land.

Our world is a dry and thirsty place, unable to provide deep contentment, true peace, or lasting joy. Nothing in this world can quench our souls' deepest longings. Money, fame, material possessions...even our families can't sustain us. God alone refreshes our souls. Jesus said, "Whoever drinks of this water will thirst again, but whoever drinks of the water that I shall give him will never thirst" (John 4:13-14 NKJV). David knew this and knew what to do: "So I have looked for You" (Psalm 63:2 NKJV). David knew he could find fulfillment, satisfaction, contentment, love, and acceptance in God alone.

How can you develop your thirst for God?

In what ways does God satisfy your soul?

O God, thank you for your living water and for always sustaining and refreshing me, even in a dry and thirsty land.

—Aaron Baddeley

Scripture Reading: Psalm 63:8 NKJV

My soul follows close behind You; Your right hand upholds me.

In this simple yet powerful verse, David describes the way he followed God's lead and relied completely upon him.

The Bible often reports that David "inquired of the Lord." He entrusted every area of his life to God, looking to God for protection from enemies, provision of everything he needed, guidance when making decisions, and victory in battle.

As we saw in yesterday's reading, David also followed God simply because he desired God. Another psalmist felt the same way: "Better is one day in your courts than a thousand elsewhere" (Psalm 84:10).

What does following close behind God entail for you?

In what way has God upheld you?

God, I admit that sometimes I've been a straggler, lagging far behind you. Thank you for waiting for me, drawing me to yourself, and upholding me with your right hand.

—Aaron Baddeley

Scripture Reading: Job 5:9 NCV

God does wonders that cannot be understood; he does so many miracles they cannot be counted.

We know of a few of Jesus's miracles—raising Lazarus from the dead, turning water to wine, feeding a crowd of thousands with one boy's lunch, calming the storm, casting out demons...

Might we see miracles every day if only we opened our eyes? Or have we adopted a worldview that rules out the supernatural? The New Testament teaches that Christ holds all things together (Colossians 1:17) by his powerful word (Hebrews 1:3). How's that for a miracle!

We also read that every good and perfect gift is from God (James 1:17). Perhaps our definition of miracles is too small. God is active in the world today. Miracles are surely happening all around us. The question is, are we noticing?

Think of some ways God has blessed your life. Thank God for these gifts.

Are you trusting God for a miracle, such as physical healing, financial provision, or a relational breakthrough? Thank God in advance for being a God of miracles.

Heavenly Father, help me to see your hand at work everywhere I go today.

—Davis Love III

We live in a world that puts people in their place. People who are willing to pay for extra services receive special boarding times on flights, unique privileges at car rental companies, credit cards that come with concierge hotlines, and the finest rooms at hotels. These can be tremendous blessings, but they can also make us feel a little more important than the next guy.

God calls us to be like Jesus, who did not consider equality with God something to be grasped. Instead, he became an ordinary person, just like us. In fact, the Creator of the universe came to us as a helpless baby, lived as a humble servant, and ultimately died as the victim of an unjust execution. He didn't consider himself too important to be with us, to be like us, to suffer for us.

How can we flesh this out? Enjoy people! Every single person you see today was created by God and for his pleasure. Each one is a gift. Pay attention to the people you meet, talk with them, pray for them, and encourage them! Have fun with them!

In the past few days, have you taken a few extra moments simply to enjoy being with someone?

Each person you meet is a gift from God. Whom might you enjoy being with today?

God, forgive me for brushing past people without recognizing what a gift each one is. Save me from feeling superior, and help me to find the treasure in the folks I meet.

—Davis Love III

This book was born out of The Player's Devotional, a 2010–2013 series of books that contained devotions for players to read before heading out into a day of competition. Many of the original contributors were Young Life staff, leaders, and friends. The proceeds from these books helped send kids from all over the world to weeklong Young Life summer camps. The proceeds from this book will do the same.

What is Young Life?

Young Life doesn't start with a program. It starts with adults who are concerned enough about kids to go to them, on their turf and in their culture, building bridges of authentic friendship. These relationships don't happen overnight—they take time, patience, trust, and consistency.

So Young Life leaders log many hours with kids—where they are, as they are. We listen to their stories and learn what's important to them because we genuinely care about their joys, triumphs, heartaches, and setbacks. We love kids regardless of their responses.

We believe in the power of presence. Kids' lives are dramatically influenced when caring adults come alongside them, sharing God's love with them. Because their Young Life leaders believe in them, they begin to see that their lives have great worth, meaning, and purpose.

This is the first step of a lifelong journey. The choices they make today, based on God's love for them, will help guide their future decisions about careers, marriages, and families—all ripples from the time when Young Life leaders took time to reach out and enter their world.

You can find out more at **www.younglife.org.**

Eric Scofield
CDO, Young Life